Fabian Gieseke

Minimum Wages and Youth Employment

European Evidence and Potential Impact on Germany

Review of Essential Economic Aspects

Volume 2

Minimum Wages and Youth Employment

European Evidence and Potential Impact on Germany

by

Fabian Gieseke

SOCIETAS 2014

Bibliographic information published by the Deutsche Nationalbibliothek

The Deutsche Nationalbibliothek lists this publication in the Deutsche Nationalbibliografie; detailed bibliographic data are available in the Internet at http://dnb.dnb.de.

Bibliographische Information der Deutschen Nationalbibliothek

Die Deutsche Nationalbibliothek verzeichnet diese Publikation in der deutschen Nationalbibliographie; detaillierte bibliographische Daten sind im Internet über <http://dnb.ddb.de> abrufbar.

Societas Verlagsgesellschaft KG, Jena, 2014
Alle Rechte vorbehalten / All rights reserved

ISBN 978-3-94420-17-2

www.societas-verlag.de
www.societas-publishers.com

Inhaltsverzeichnis

List of Abbreviations 9

List of Symbols 11

1 Introduction 13
   1.1 Problem and Aim of the Thesis 13
   1.2 Structure of the Thesis 14

2 Theoretical Impacts of Minimum Wages and the Relevance of the Youth Labor Market 17
   2.1 The Theory of Minimum Wages 17
      2.1.1 Definition of the Term "Minimum Wage" . . . 17
      2.1.2 The Neoclassical Model 19
      2.1.3 The Monopsony Model 21
      2.1.4 Oligopsony and Monopsonistic Competition . 24
      2.1.5 A Two Sector Model 26
      2.1.6 Heterogeneous Workers 28
      2.1.7 The Efficiency Wage Theory 30
      2.1.8 Lagged Adjustment Theory 32
      2.1.9 Discussion of the Results 33
   2.2 Youth Labor Markets and Youth Unemployment . . 38
      2.2.1 Definition of the Terms 40
      2.2.2 Factors Influencing Youth Unemployment . . 41
      2.2.3 Consequences of Youth Unemployment 43

3 European Evidence about Minimum Wage Impacts on Youths 49
   3.1 Measurement Methods and Principles of the Literature Review 50

	3.1.1	Strengths and Weaknesses of different Measurement Methods	50
	3.1.2	Literature Review: Country Selection	54
	3.1.3	Principles and Methods of the Literature Review	55
3.2	France		61
	3.2.1	Situation	61
	3.2.2	Effect on Young Workers' Employment	62
3.3	Spain, Greece and Portugal		64
	3.3.1	Situation	64
	3.3.2	Effect on Young Workers' Employment	66
3.4	Belgium and the Netherlands		68
	3.4.1	Situation	68
	3.4.2	Effect on Young Workers' Employment	70
3.5	United Kingdom and the United States of America .		72
	3.5.1	Situation	72
	3.5.2	Effect on Young Workers' Employment	74
3.6	Discussion of the Results		76

4 Potential Impact of MWs on the Youth Labor Market in Germany 79

4.1	Current Situation in Germany		79
	4.1.1	Minimum Wages and Collective Agreements in Certain Sectors	79
	4.1.2	The Youth Labor Market and Youth Unemployment	81
	4.1.3	State of Affairs in the German Minimum Wage Debate	83
4.2	Simulation of Impacts of a potential Minimum Wage on the Youth Labor Market and Empirical Evidence from Germany		88
	4.2.1	Empirical Evidence from German Simulations and Studies	88
	4.2.2	Applied Method of the self-conducted Simulation	90
	4.2.3	Results of the self-conducted Simulation . . .	92
	4.2.4	Critical Assessment of the self-conducted Simulation	95
4.3	Modifications within the System of Minimum Wages		96
	4.3.1	Subminimum Wages for Young Workers . . .	96
	4.3.2	Sector specific Minimum Wages	98
	4.3.3	Minimum Wages set by a Commission of Experts	98

5 Conclusion	. . . .	101
Appendix	. . . .	105
List of References	. . . .	131
List of Tables	. . . .	151
List of Figures	. . . .	153

List of Abbreviations

AEntG	Arbeitnehmer-Entsendegesetz
BAP	Beschäftigtenpanel
BDA	Confederation of German Employers' Associations
CDU	Christian Democratic Union
CME	coordinated market economy
CPI	consumer price index
DGB	German trade union federation (Deutscher Gewerkschaftsbund)
DIW	German Institute for Economic Research
EAP	Economically Active Population
ECB	European Central Bank
EEAG	European Economic Advisory Group
EU	European Union
FDP	Free Democratic Party
GLS	Gehalts- und Lohnstrukturerhebung
HWWI	Hamburg Institute of International Economics
i.a.	inter alia
IAB	German Institute for Employment Research
ifo Institut	Institute for Economic Research
IfW	Kiel Institute for the World Economy
ILO	International Labour Organization
ILS	Association of Instore and Logistic Services
IMF	International Monetary Fund

LME	liberal market economy
LPC	Low Pay Commission
MW	minimum wage
NEET	not in employment, education or training
NGG	Food, Beverages and Catering Union
NGO	non-governmental organization
NMW	National Minimum Wage
OECD	Organization for Economic Co-operation and Development
PPP	purchasing power parity
RMMMG	Revenu Minimum Mensuel Moyen Garantie
SMI	Salario Minimo Interprofesional
SMIC	Salaire Minimum Interprofessionnel de Croissance
SMN	Salario Minimo Nacional
SOEP	German Socio-Economic Panel
SPD	Social Democratic Party of Germany
UK	United Kingdom
USA	United States of America
USD	United States Dollar
Ver.di	United Services Union
VOKA	Vlaams Economisch Verbond
VSE	Verdienst- und Strukturerhebung
ZEW	Centre for European Economic Research

List of Symbols

CS		covered sector
D		labor demand
D_c		labor demand in covered sector
D_u		labor demand in uncovered sector
E		employment
E_0		initial employment level
E_1		employment level after MW introduction
E_2		supplied labor
i		company i
MC		marginal cost
MC'		marginal cost after MW introduction
P		productive sector
S		labor supply
S_u		labor supply in uncovered sector before MW introduction
S'_u		labor supply in uncovered sector after MW introduction
UP		unproductive sector
US		uncovered sector
W		wage (gross labor cost)
W_m		minimum wage
W_0		wage in period 0
W^*		competitive wage
η		elasticity of labor demand

1 Introduction

1.1 Problem and Aim of the Thesis

"Poor despite work. Germany needs the minimum wage" [1]
(DGB, 2013)

Since 2007 political parties, labor unions and many other non-governmental organizations (NGOs) are increasingly demanding a statutory minimum wage (MW) for Germany. Furthermore a large share of the population (86%) supports the notion of a national MW, which is constantly gaining more traction (Infratest dimap, 2013). Due to increasing pressure to implement the policy, action seems very likely in the near future, especially when considering the outcome of the federal election on September 22nd which has reinforced this probability.

However, this development took place despite the massive resistance of many German and international economists who repeatedly warn that a MW would have adverse effects on the labor market and a particular large negative impact on youth employment. The view that young persons are more likely to be affected by a statutory MW is confirmed by a large amount of empirical research (e.g. Ghellab, 1998) and furthermore supported through analysis of the labor markets of foreign countries. According to many economists (e.g. Sinn, 2008) the enormous youth unemployment rates of countries like France, Spain or Greece are at least partly caused by MWs which were set too high. Some governments even started to lower MW levels (e.g. Greece) or discuss reductions of the subminimum wages for youths (e.g. France) while

---

[1] Original: "Arm trotz Arbeit. Deutschland braucht den Mindestlohn." Title of the current campaign of the German trade union federation (DGB) which supports the nationwide introduction of a minimum wage of EUR 8.50.

other countries launched programs which aim to assist young persons in finding employment (e.g. UK).

Proponents of a MW in Germany reject these arguments and claim that wage floors would protect low-wage workers and combat rising levels of inequality and poverty (Rycx and Kampelmann, 2012, p. 5). Additionally, they refer to studies from the United States and the United Kingdom which showed positive employment effects of MWs for young workers (e.g. Card and Krueger, 1994).

So far there are no studies or simulations, which deal with the potential consequences of wage floors in Germany and have focused particularly on young persons. This is hard to understand given the fact that youth unemployment brings not only large negative consequences for the affected individual but also for the wider society. Therefore the smooth functioning of the transition process between school and work is of high importance because joblessness among youths can lead to further unemployment in their later career, thus containing a high financial burden for the economy. Currently Germany faces the lowest rate of unemployment among teenagers and young adults in the European Union (Eurostat, 2013a). Whether the introduction of a statutory MW could change this situation is uncertain because much cannot be answered due to a lack of simulations and studies. This thesis tries to fill this gap and therefore analyzes the following research question:

> *"What are the potential impacts of a legal minimum wage on the youth labor market in Germany and how can experiences made by other European countries help to deal with this question?"*

1.2 Structure of the Thesis

To answer this question the thesis is structured as follows. Chapter 2 sets the theoretical background and analyzes different models which try to estimate the potential employment effects of a MW implementation. This should answer the question of what predictions concerning the introduction of a wage floor can be made from a theoretical perspective. Furthermore, other factors that have influence on the labor market for young workers apart from the MW will be presented. The chapter concludes with an overview of the various consequences of youth unemployment.

Chapter 3 considers the question what happened in other European countries' youth labor markets when MWs were introduced or changed and how this could be measured. In this context it provides first an overview about the most common approaches which are used to evaluate MW impacts and describes their strengths and weaknesses. Before beginning with the analysis of the empirical evidence in 3.2, a brief explanation is given how the literature review was conducted and why certain countries were included into the review. Afterwards, the following four sections deal with different countries by starting with a short summary about how MWs are set in this country and the way in which they apply to youths, as well as how the current economic situation on the nation's youth labor market can be characterized. For each country the most relevant studies were selected and their results briefly summarized. Despite the fact that this chapter focuses on empirical evidence from European countries, studies concerning the United States are also included because they are often cited to show that MWs can indeed have positive effects on youth employment.

Chapter 4 focuses on the situation in Germany and estimates potential impacts of a MW introduction on the status of young employees. Before estimating these impacts, section 4.1 describes the state of affairs in the German MW debate and outlines the current situation for young persons in the labor market. The following estimation is based on two approaches. The first approach contains an analysis of simulations and studies which deal with effects of sectoral MWs in some German industries while the second approach tries to calculate potential employment impacts for young workers with the help of a self-conducted simulation. Therefore it uses constant elasticities of labor demand and a data set provided by the German Socio-Economic Panel (SOEP, 2011). The chapter concludes with an overview of modifications within the system of MWs which aim to mitigate the negative employment effects.

Finally, the thesis ends with a conclusion which contains a short summary about the most relevant results and an answer to the research question.

2 Theoretical Impacts of Minimum Wages and the Relevance of the Youth Labor Market

As described in the introduction, most of the countries in the European Union and in the OECD area use MWs to regulate the labor market. This kind of policy is criticized by many economists who blame MWs as being at least partly responsible for the high youth unemployment rates in the EU because they would act as impediments for young people when making the transition from school to work. This chapter deals with the question why this might be the case and presents different views which model the potential impacts of an introduction of a statutory MW on the (youth) labor market. Furthermore, this chapter shows why unemployment among youths is a serious problem and presents consequences of high rates of joblessness for the society as well as for the affected individual. Before that, section 2.2 illustrates the characteristics of the youth labor market and explains what other factors apart from the MW can cause youth unemployment

2.1 The Theory of Minimum Wages

2.1.1 Definition of the Term "Minimum Wage"

According to the OECD (1998), a minimum wage (MW) is the smallest amount of compensation employees must receive for performing labor. MWs can be set on an hourly, daily, weekly or monthly basis, which makes a cross-country comparison of their levels complicated. Additionally there are huge differences in the way how many different minimum levels are set within one country. Many countries vary by age, across regions, occupation and industry, duration of employment and size of firm (Dolado et al., 1996, p. 321). In some countries a workers minimum can be based on their professional experience (Greece and Belgium), their professional qualifications (Czech Republic and Luxembourg) or their family and marital status (Luxembourg and Greece) (OECD, 1998, p. 32). Furthermore countries vary in the way the MW is set. Dolado et al. (1996, p. 321) distinguish between five main types:

a) MW is determined by the government (possibly in consultation with employers and unions)[2]: i.a. France, Spain, the Netherlands, Portugal

b) MW is set as part of national collective bargains: i.a. Belgium, Denmark, Greece

c) Different MWs can be set in sectoral collective agreements which are generally extended to companies who were not participating at the original agreements: i.a. Austria, Germany, Italy

d) Collective agreements can cover effectively a whole industry and generally contain wage floors without any formal provision for extension to non-signatory employers: i.a Finland, Norway, Sweden

e) MWs can be set in selected low-paying industries: i.a. Ireland

Once set, the criterion for adjusting the MW rate varies between countries. For example a MW may be reset according to the evolution of the average wage or the inflation rate and sometimes even according to criteria thought to reflect the impact of the MW itself on the labor market (Cahuc and Zylberberg, 2004, p. 715).

However the biggest difference between national minimum wages is the level of the minimum relative to average wages and therefore the importance of the MW in the wage determination process. Cahuc and Zylberberg (2004, p. 715) point out that measuring the real level of the MW may be insufficient in comparisons between countries with diverse productivity levels. For the purpose of making international comparisons possible, the relative size of the MW is often measured by the Kaitz index, which is in its most basic version defined as the ratio

---

[2]Often also referred to as statutory minimum wage or legal minimum wage.

of the MW to the average wage or the median wage of the working population (Schulten, 2013, p. 130; Kaitz, 1970).[3]

2.1.2 The Neoclassical Model

The neoclassical model is also known under "Simple Supply-Demand Model" and thus the most basic model analyzing the impact of minimum wages on employment and unemployment. The model assumes a single competitive labor market with homogenous workers who are all covered by the MW. Assuming homogenous workers implies that all workers have the same skills and also the levels of effort are identical, which are given exogenously. Furthermore the model neglects a time horizon meaning that adjustment processes to changes in the wage rate are happening immediately (Brown et al., 1982a, p. 4).

Figure 1 illustrates the situation starting with no minimum wages. The initial employment level E_0 is determined by supply and demand while the equilibrium wage rate is denoted by W_0. After introduction of the MW, the wage rate increases to W_m and employment falls to E_1 because of the decrease in labor demand. The fall in labor demand requires the assumption that the demand function for labor is negatively inclined. The proportional reduction in employment (E_0-E_1) is equal to the proportional wage increase (W_m-W_0) times the elasticity of labor demand. Moreover the number of workers who want to work at W_m rises and exceeds the number of jobs available. This can be assumed if the supply curve is positively inclined as depicted in Figure 1 (Welch, 1974, pp. 294-295). The excess supply of labor at the new MW can be clearly seen (E_2-E_1) but Brown et al. (1982a, p. 4) emphasize that this excess supply does not correspond to the official measure of unemployment. Not everyone who is willing to work at W_m is also actively searching for an employment contract and those who are not actively searching are not included in the official unemployment statistics. Nevertheless, Cahuc and Zylberberg (2004, p. 718) point out that classical unemployment arises which can only be reabsorbed by lowering the MW. The employment loss from a given MW depends on the elasticity of labor demand and will be larger given the more elastic the demand curve is (Dolado et al., 1996, p. 328). The described negative effects of a MW on employment result in a

---

[3] See chapter 3.1.1 for a more detailed description of the Kaitz index and potential weaknesses in the measurement of the relevance of a MW.

real labor market formed by a combination of two elements. Firstly the substitution effect, which means that firms substitute skilled-labor for unskilled-labor or use more capital than labor since labor becomes relatively more expensive because of the higher wage W_m. The second element is the scale effect which results from the decrease of sales due to cost increases, leading to a reduction in the use of both input factors, capital and labor (Ghellab, 1998, p. 3).

Figure: 1: Impact of a MW in the Neoclassical Model

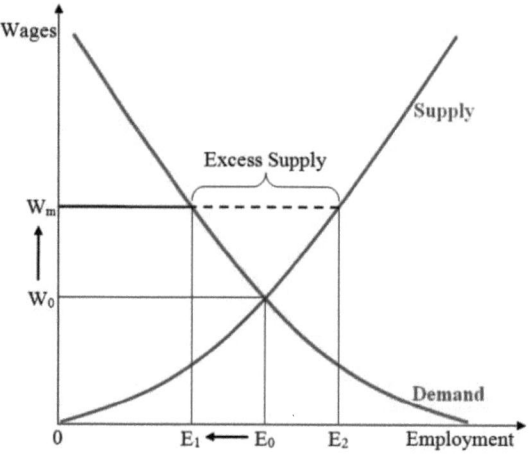

(Source: Adapted from Welch, 1974, p. 295)

By adopting this model to reality, those workers who are affected by unemployment are most likely young or low-qualified people. Croucher and White (2011, p. 12) state that younger workers will likely be replaced by older workers which have a number of competitive advantages. Due to their greater life and work experience as well as their industry-specific knowledge older employees might have a higher productivity and need less training and less supervision than younger persons. Nevertheless, the authors also underline positive attributes on the side of younger workers. According to Croucher and White (2011, p. 12) younger employees are usually characterized by a higher time and task flexibility. Hashimoto (1982) adds that neoclassical theory predicts not only that a MW will have a negative impact on employment but also on training. On the one hand a MW will prevent workers from finding a job because of the negative employment effects, meaning that they also will not receive any on-the-job-training. Additionally, those who find employment are less likely to receive any training as their employer cannot offset the costs for on-the-job-training by offering a lower wage. In the long run this can lead to negative impacts on innovation and productivity.

Many authors have criticized this model because of its restrictive assumptions. Card and Krueger (1997, pp. 356-357) claim that the model completely ignores heterogeneity in the labor force and therefore that firms hire workers at a variety of different wage rates and skill levels. The authors underline their critique by stating that some workers earn more than others within a firm and even within a relatively homogenous group such as teenagers. Ghellab (1998, p. 3) adds that labor markets are neither homogenous nor restrained by strict competitive rules. According to him the notion of "equilibrium", on which the neoclassical model is based, does not seem to reflect the complex and dynamic nature of contemporary labor markets. Furthermore, the model incorrectly assumes no lagged effects of a MW introduction and perfect information of employers and employees which cannot be found in reality (OECD, 1998, p. 43).

2.1.3 The Monopsony Model

The first economist who used the term "monopsony" was Robinson (1969), who constructed the term analogous to monopoly. While monopolies are perceived as cases where a single seller is confronted with many buyers, monopsonies refer to cases where a single buyer faces a market with many sellers. Similar to a monopolist who faces a downward sloping demand curve for his product and can set the price in order to maximize his profits, the monopsonist is confronted with an upward slopping supply curve for the good being sold and can also set the price.

Stigler (1946) was the first author who realized that a binding moderate MW in a monopsonistic situation could lead to an increase in employment. Stigler explains this phenomenon with the "company town" in which a single firm dominates. This situation could be found in coal mining communities in rural areas especially in earlier times (Ashenfelter et al., 2010, p. 2). Being the only firm in the labor market that demands labor, is giving the employer absolute market power. Similar to a monopolist in the output market, the monopsonist maximizes its profits by choosing the lowest wage possible to attract a sufficient number of workers to produce at a desired level. The monopsonist firm remunerates every employee with potentially less than its marginal productivity (see wage W_0 in the monopsony model in Figure 2). In doing so, the company produces at minimal costs (Cahuc and Zylberberg, 2004, p. 719). After introducing a MW, the company becomes a price-taker and the wage rate rises from W_0 to the minimum rate W_m, leading also to an increase in employment (from E_0 to E_1) as long as the MW is lower than the competitive wage (W^*) (Moser and Stähler, 2009, p. 2). Further increases in the wage floor higher than W^* would reduce employment below the competitive level (Brown et al., 1982a, p. 5).

Card and Krueger (1997, p. 378) give an intuitive explanation for the described positive employment effect. According to them a monopsonistic company maintains a positive stock of vacancies in the monopsonistic equilibrium and would gladly hire additional employees at the offered wage (W_0). However, the firm would have to pay a higher salary to its existing employees to attract more workers which it is not willing to do. In such a situation a MW raises the recruiting rate and fills some of the firm's vacancies. Nevertheless, Welch (1974, p. 298) points out that it is extremely difficult to determine an optimum wage floor because a exceedingly high MW will lead to a situation in which the firm has to fire workers to raise the marginal revenue product of labor up to the level of the minimum.

Figure: 2: The MW impact in the Neoclassical and in the Monopsony Model

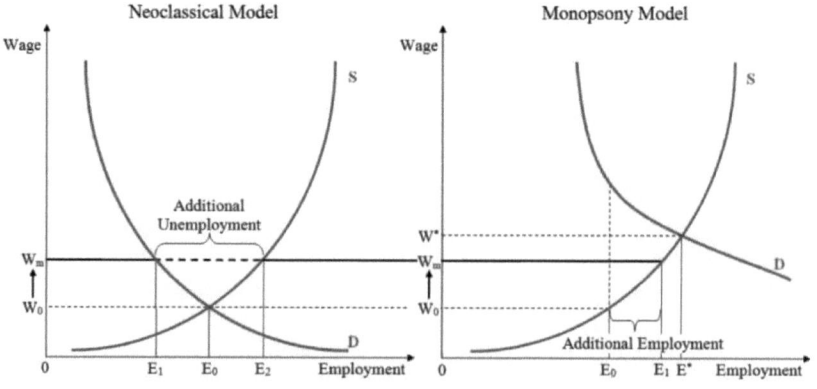

(Source: Adapted from Bauer and Schmidt, 2007, p. 6)

As described above a monopsonistic situation can occur because of missing competition in a local labor market but more generally due to labor market imperfections in the way of segmentation, differentiation and lack of transparency. These kinds of imperfections can lead to market power even for smaller firms. To obtain such conditions, high market entry barriers are needed as well as serious mobility impairments for workers (Franz et al., 2008, p. 9). Sinn (2008, p. 59) adds that monopsonies can also exist if employees are overly specialized and only qualified to work for one company in the local labor market. In general three sources of imperfections are possible which can give companies the opportunity to pay workers less than their actual contribution to the firm. According to Metcalf (2007) these are the absence of perfect information on alternative jobs, material and social costs of changing the employer and different preferences by workers (the social environment, distance to the job and hours of labor).

Similar to the neoclassical model, the monopsony model is as well highly criticized. Many economists see it as a theoretical curiosity with limited practical relevance because it would imply a situation with one single employer or a cartel-like union (Bhaskar and To, 1999, p. 1; Raddatz and Wolf, 2007, p. 7). Machin and Manning (1992) underline this critique by stating that employees who are generally most affected by a MW are low-paid and unskilled workers who are usually employed in small firms. Furthermore Card and Krueger (1997, p. 373) add that in markets for relatively unskilled workers the buyers of labor are typically small companies (e.g. retail outlets, service stations, restaurants) and therefore each firm employs only a tiny friction of unskilled employees in their local markets meaning that their degree of monopsony power is rather negligible. Other authors conclude that purely monopsonistic situations are very uncommon and there is no evidence to suggest the extent of this phenomenon (Welch, 1974, p. 12; Cahuc and Zylberberg, 2004, p. 720).

In contrast to theses beliefs other economists suggest that at least some companies and sectors would have a significant degree of monopsony power (Card and Krueger, 1997, p. 379). Brown et al. (1982a, p. 5) and Ashenfelter et al. (2010, pp. 8-9) detected in their studies some allocative problems associated with monopsonistic exploitation and thus found a range of remarkable evidence to suggest that labor markets are far from being competitive. Dolado et al. (1996, p. 330) support these views by summarizing that the important features of the monopsony model will be reproduced in any situation where employers have at least some influence over the wage setting process. According to them it is the neoclassical model with its perfect competition assumption that is the extreme and implausible outcome. For that reason Fitzenberger (2009, pp. 86-87) refuses both models and is convinced that the situation in reality and especially in Germany is best represented by the model of monopsonistic competition.

2.1.4 Oligopsony and Monopsonistic Competition

As discussed above traditional monopsony is probably an unrealistic case because firms obviously compete with one another at least to some extent. The models of oligopsony and monopsonistic competition can be located somewhere in the middle ground between perfect competition and monopsony. While oligopsony represents a situation in which employer market power exists despite competition with other firms, monopsonistic competition is oligopsony with free entries and exits which drives company profits down to zero (Bhaskar et al., 2002, p. 156). Market power for every single employer and the possibility to choose wages arises due to different jobs as well as their different non-wage characteristics, and despite the fact that single companies only employ a small fraction of the labor force (Bhaskar and To, 1999, p. 190).

Figure 3 shows the effect of a MW on a labor market with monopsonistic competition. Fixed costs in production and a less than perfectly elastic supply curve are assumed since firms are competing for workers (Moser and Stähler, 2009, p. 2). The result is similar to the case of monopsony where a price floor like the MW prevents a profit-maximizing monopsonist from reducing the quantity of labor by cutting the wage as much as this company desires. Without a MW, the employment rate and the equilibrium wage is depicted by E_0 and W_0. After imposing a MW (W_m) the marginal cost of labor is now W_m and the employment level rises to E_1, implying a growth in employment of E_1-E_0 (Stigler, 1946).

In case of an oligopsony or monopsonistic competition the effect of a MW changes. Since many employers compete for workers, the labor supply curve (S) faced by company i also depends on its rival wage rates. After introducing a MW all competitors have to raise their wage to the minimum, leading on an increase in labor market competition so that the labor supply curve faced by company i shifts to the left (S').

Consequently marginal cost of labor shifts from MC to MC', leading to an employment rate of E_2. Furthermore, the binding MW reduces profits of the competitors and forces some employers to exit the labor market. Obviously these employer exits have a negative impact on total employment through a loss of jobs from the exiting firms. Figure 3 illustrates the difference between a MW under monopsony and monopsonistic competition, showing that the potential increase of the employment rate is higher under a situation with monopsony (Bhaskar et al., 2002, pp. 168-169).

Figure: 3: MW and Employment under Monopsonistic Competition

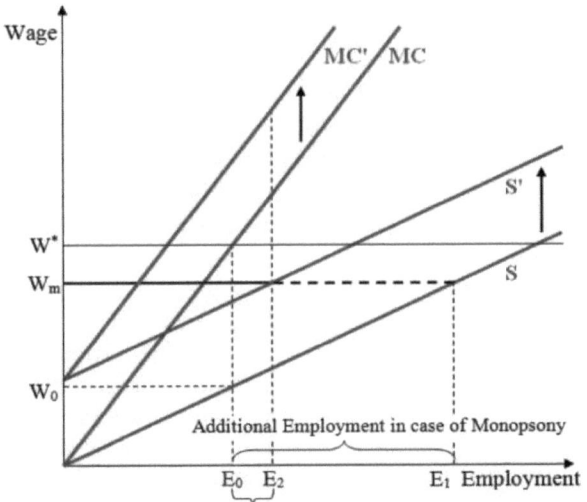

(Source: Adapted from Bhaskar et al., 2002, p. 169)

In summary, a MW under monopsonistic competition has two countervailing effects. The first one is the "monopsonistic competition" or "oligopsony" effect leading to an employment increase. The second one is the employment-reducing "exit" effect. Thus, the overall effect of a MW on employment depends on which of these two effects dominates. Therefore Bhaskar et al. (2002, p. 169) conclude that a moderately set MW above the market wage (W_0) may have a negative or a positive impact on total employment, however the size of this impact will generally be small due to the two countervailing forces. Nevertheless, the authors state that even if employment falls, the overall employment effect will be smaller under monopsonistic competition than under perfect competition in the neoclassical model.

2.1.5 A Two Sector Model

According to Brown et al. (1982a, p. 7) many countries have a MW which does not cover the whole population. The same is true for Germany and this is the reason why it is reasonable to consider a model with incomplete coverage.

Figure 4 illustrates a situation with two sectors. One of it is covered by a MW (W_m), the other is not. After introducing a MW in the covered sector (CS), the initial wage rate (W_0) increases to the minimum level (W_m). Afterwards the covered sector reacts to the MW as it would if coverage would have been universal (Welch, 1974, pp. 311-312). Due to the higher wage some employees in the CS lose their jobs and those who are displaced by the increased wage move to the uncovered sector (US). This raises the labor supply for the uncovered sector and shifts the supply curve downwards (from S_u to S'_u) which results in a wage fall (from W_0 to W_1 and an increase in the employment level from E_0 to E_1. Nevertheless, Welch (1974, p. 315) emphasizes that employees displaced from the covered sector do not automatically find new employment in the uncovered sector. More likely some of them and some of those who were originally employed in the uncovered sector will quit the labor force since the offered wages in the US (W_1) are now lower than their reservation wages. Because of these circumstances Brown et al. (1982a, pp. 7-8) conclude that the overall MW effect on total employment depends on the elasticity of labor supply to wages, the elasticity of labor demand, the reservation wages of those who are not employed in the covered sector as well as the relative size of the covered sector. Ghellab (1998, p. 4) states that these elements make an analysis even more complex and show that the relationship between the employment rate and MWs is not as easy as it is described in the basic neoclassical model.

2.1 The Theory of Minimum Wages   27

Figure: 4: Impact of a MW in a Two-Sector Model

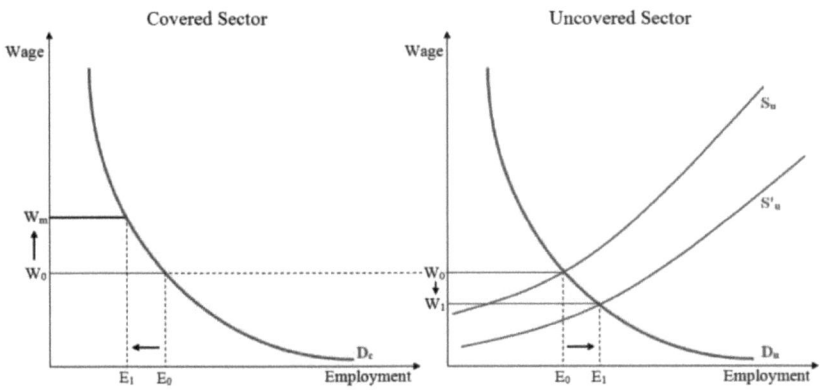

(Source: Adapted from Welch, 1974, p. 312)

In the analyzed model above, the two sectors have only differed in the fact that one of them was covered by a MW while the other one was not. Moser and Stähler (2009) change this setting slightly and assume differences in the sector productivity.[4] They label one sector productive (P) while the other one is referred to as the unproductive sector (UP). These productivity differences are not caused by different skill levels of the employees but rather by economies with regional or sectoral varieties, where the same type of worker can be employed in either sector (e.g. agricultural vs. industrial).

Wages in the productive sector are higher than those in the unproductive sector. To lower the wage gap and in order to correct the "unfair" wage payments in the unproductive sector, a fictional government imposes a MW in the unproductive sector which is still smaller than (or, at most, equal to) the competitive wage bargained in the productive sector (Moser and Stähler, 2009, p. 11). In contrast to the results from Welch (1974), Moser and Stähler (2009, p. 20) come to the conclusion that the MW clearly reduces job creation and employment only in the not covered productive sector, while its impact on employment in the unproductive sector is ambiguous. The authors ex-

---

[4] Furthermore Moser and Stähler (2009, p. 6) assume an exogenously given rate of job destruction and free entry of vacancies. Unemployment in this model is the residual state, meaning that workers whose employment in either the unproductive or productive sector ends will flow back into unemployment.

plain this by the fact that the MW in the covered unproductive sector increases the jobless persons' outside options because any employment in the unproductive sector yields a higher salary now. This increased outside option improves the bargaining position of workers in P leading to a demand for higher wages and a situation in which employers are less willing to hire additional workers and instead fire employees because of the increased wage. This reduced job creation in P decreases the likelihood that workers in UP will find employment in P and thus leave sector UP. This situation may trigger job creation in UP but on the other hand the incentive for job creation in UP decreases because of the higher wage costs. Therefore the total employment effect in UP depends on which of the described effects dominates.

In summary it can be stated that a MW in a two-sector model can, under certain circumstances, even raise the overall level of employment. But even if this is the case, it can only be achieved at the cost of less productive employment and with higher levels of "unproductive employment" (Moser and Stähler, 2009, p. 16).

Similar to the neoclassical model, the two-sector models is also criticized for not taking into account the imperfections of markets such as the lack of information on job opportunities faced by workers (Ghellab, 1998, p. 5). Furthermore, the model neglects the heterogeneous nature of workers, instead assuming that all employees in both sectors are homogenous (Card and Krueger, 1997, p. 364).

2.1.6 Heterogeneous Workers

Two Types of Labor

The simplest heterogeneous-worker model allows for two types of labor: unskilled workers (L_1) and skilled workers (L_2). Both are imperfect substitutes for each other and for non-labor inputs (e.g. capital). An introduction of a MW affects only the wage for unskilled labor (W_1) and not the wage for skilled labor (W_2). As described in the models before, employment of employees whose wages are affected by the MW will fall which in this case are the unskilled workers. The impact of MW on total employment (L_1+L_2) remains ambiguous. Depending on the degree of complementarities between skilled and unskilled labor, the cross-substitution effect between the two types of labor could offset the decrease in employment of L_1. However, total employment will decline with an increasing unskilled wage if non-labor inputs are a substitute for unskilled workers (Brown et al., 1982a, pp. 14-15; Card and Krueger, 1997, p. 360).

Continuous Types of Labor

As seen in reality, wage distributions tend to be relatively smooth which is why discrete types of workers with discrete wage levels do not fit to the empirics. To analyze continuous types of labor Welch (1969) uses a human capital model which supposes that different employees possess various amounts of human capital. The labor market in this model is characterized by a single wage rate for one unit of human capital, implying that each worker receives a wage that equals the product of his human capital stock and the price of one unit of human capital.

Figure 5 illustrates the impact of an imposed MW on the wage distribution. As depicted in the figure, the MW shifts the entire distribution of wages to the right which reflects a raise in the market price of human capital. Furthermore the distribution of wages is truncated on the left of the MW. The increase in the market price of human capital will be bigger, the lower the elasticity of human capital demand (labor demand) is. With less than perfectly inelastic demand, the increase in the MW will lower the employment of low-wage workers and will lead to a rise in wages for all other workers as shown in Figure 5. Employees whose salaries are the furthest below the MW are most likely to lose their jobs, while workers who earn wages just above the MW are likely to gain higher wages or keep at least their employment (Card and Krueger, 1997, pp. 362-363).

Figure: 5: Theoretical Wage Distribution with and without a MW

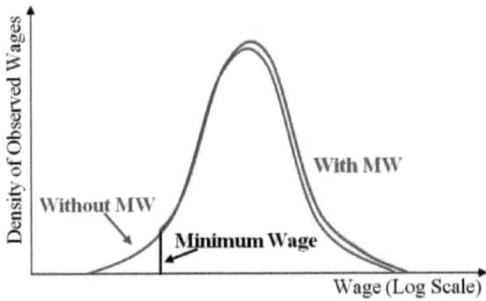

(Source: Adapted from Card and Krueger, 1997, p. 362)

Card and Krueger (1997, p. 363) admit that the biggest weakness of the model is the prediction that wages will increase by the same amount for all workers who were originally earning more than the MW.

2.1.7 The Efficiency Wage Theory

This theory is based on the assumption that an increase in real wages due to an established MW can lead through various mechanisms to higher labor productivity which could even compensate for the negative impact on total employment. Some of the dimensions on which the efficiency wage theory is based on are described below:

Shirking and Sociological Dimension

Since it is very difficult to measure effort of employees, many workers find incentives to do less work than agreed in the contract. These shirking or moral hazard can be reduced with the help of a MW which is set above the market equilibrium level. The higher wage increases the cost of losing the job and motivates the worker to increase personal effort and to work harder (OECD, 1998, p. 44).

The sociological dimension is based on the concepts of reciprocity and fairness. Reciprocity implies that people are willing to sacrifice their own goods to help those who are being kind to them but are also willing to sacrifice their own goods to punish someone who was unkind to them (Rabin, 1993). In this context a very low wage could be seen by the employee as unfair or unkind behavior, which could lead to shirking or even sabotage, while a wage increase due to an introduction of a MW could be seen as a positive signal which might increase commitment and solidarity to the employer (Börsch-Supan, 2008, p. 37). According to Metcalf (2007) these kinds of behavioral changes by the employees could lead to positive impacts on a firm's productivity.

In contrast to the aforementioned ideas, Brown et al. (1982a, pp. 5-6) believe that employers are rather responsible for rises in overall productivity. From their perspective a MW "shocks" firms into greater productivity if they are not able to minimize costs or to transfer cost increases onto consumers in the form of higher prices. This is often achieved through an increase in the employer's expectations and demand for higher levels of productivity from their employees, which is accompanied by the threat of unemployment if standards are not met.

Human Capital Investment Dimension

A MW raises the wage level within a sector or an industry and therefore increases the incentive to get a job as well as to keep a job in this industry. Low-productivity workers outside the labor market try to invest in more education or training in order to raise their productivity level and to obtain employment while low-productivity workers inside the labor force do the same to reduce the risk of getting fired (OECD, 1998, p. 44).

On the other hand employers can try to increase their employees' productivity by providing a higher quality and quantity of training and by encouraging more efficient practices (Bertola et al., 2013, p. 81). Additionally, restraints on wage competition can reduce the fear of employers that a well trained worker might be head-hunted by higher wage offers and allows them to invest in their apprentices' human capital accumulation (Acemoglu and Pischke, 1999).

Turnover Dimension

According to Ghellab (1998, p. 7) low-wages are associated with high job turnovers and this is again associated with the loss of company-specific knowledge, experience and skills leading to a decline in labor productivity. A higher wage rate reduces job turnovers and secures the firm from losing important human capital (OECD, 1998, p. 44).

Nutritional Dimension

This dimension fits more to the situation in developing countries and is not appropriate for the German case. A minimum subsistence wage could allow workers to eat well enough which would have a positive impact on their health situation making them able to work harder and to be more productive (Ghellab, 1998, p. 7).

Some economists claim that empirical evidence for the efficiency wage theory is rather limited and many studies show contradictory results. Lechthaler and Snower (2008, p. 43) for example state that the introduction of a MW would decrease the incentive for firms to train low-qualified employees because the reduced profitability of those workers would shorten their duration of employment. Due to this shorter duration of employment the utility of an apprenticeship for the company would be significantly reduced. Nevertheless, medium and highly-qualified workers might gain from a MW since on-the-job-training will increase for them. This is why Lechthaler and Snower conclude that a MW would harm primarily those workers who should gain from it by calculating that low-qualified workers will lose on average 11.3% of their human capital stock due to a ten percent increase in an existing MW accompanied by a sharp reduction of training. Croucher and White (2011, p. 83) emphasize that this shortened education will lead to lower salaries for the affected low-qualified workers in the long-run.

Furthermore MWs can also have a negative impact on schooling because students might be attracted by the higher wage and hence quit school to start working (Neumark and Wascher, 2010, pp. 207-208). Empirical studies about how MWs affect schooling decisions are still very rare but most of them point to negative effects (Neumark and Nizalova, 2004). Due to the described adverse effects of MWs on education and firm-provided training, Neumark and Wascher (2010, p. 223) conclude that reductions in schooling or training among teenagers and young adults could have negative long term impacts which are independent of any MW induced changes in the employment level and as a result would be more widespread than the disemployment effects.

2.1.8 Lagged Adjustment Theory

According to Card and Krueger (1997, pp. 366-367) the aforementioned models are essentially long-term models which suppose that firms can adjust to a change in the price of labor without any costs. However, in the short run most of the non-labor inputs (e.g. capital in the form of machines) may be expensive to adjust or may even be sunk. By assuming costly adjustment or sunken input factors, the employment rate of a company is unlikely to react immediately to an introduction of a MW. Instead the authors demonstrate that adaption processes will take place over the long-run since firms need some time to downsize or to exit the market. Hamermesh (1995) adds that firms are not able to adjust non-labor inputs immediately, which delays the adjustment of other inputs such as labor. For this reason the omission of lagged effects exclude longer-term substitution between labor and capital and thus further extend negative employment effects and scale effects. Card and Krueger (1997, p. 367) conclude that it is extremely important to distinguish between short-term and long-term responses to the MW. For the authors short-run (less than six months) costs of a MW introduction are borne by employers, whereas long-run costs are borne by parts of the workers, affected companies and consumers. Siebert (2008, p. 19) takes the same view and expects that adjustment processes to an MW introduction in Germany would take up to ten or even more years since companies would not only substitute capital for labor but also by relocating the whole firm abroad. The assumption of the described lagged effects is also backed by empirical evidence which indicates that effects are stronger one to two years after a MW increase than directly after or during the first year of the raise (Neumark and Wascher, 2010, p. 98).

In contrast to these views some economists take the opinion that lagged adjustments to a MW introduction are less plausible than in most other contexts where lags are routinely assumed (Brown et al., 1982a, pp. 21-22). They justify this by stating that adjustment processes can be accomplished quickly because of the higher turnover rates of MW workers and by the fact that MW increases or an introduction of a legal MW are enacted months or even years before they actually become valid. Hence, Brown et al. conclude that "leads" are as logical as "lags" and when they occur "lags" are generally very short. This opinion is also supported by Card and Krueger (1997, p. 67) who emphasize that industries which typically employ MW workers (e.g. fast food restaurants) are able to easily adapt and quickly vary their staffing levels by cutting back store hours and by allowing for longer lines so that employment effects should be visible briefly after the MW was introduced or raised.

2.1.9 Discussion of the Results

The introduction of a MW leads to a varying range of effects. In the analysis above we focused on the employment effects and on the impact on the wage levels. Table 1 summarizes the results of the different models and theories, gives additional information not mentioned in the text and lists the main points of criticism for each approach. As seen in the analysis so far and in the table, the theoretical consequences of introducing or raising MWs are far from being certain and differ from model to model. While the neoclassical model predicts the effects of unemployment and an efficiency reduction of the labor market, the monopsony model comes to a contradictory conclusion. Here a binding MW can under some circumstances increase employment and enhance the efficiency of the labor market (Brown et al., 1982a, p. 22). The remaining theories often identify other factors which are relevant to lowering the disemployment effect (e.g. additional effort from the employees, higher efficiency due to training, movements from covered to uncovered sector) but all of these mitigating effects have a welfare cost of its own. This is the reason why Brown et al. (1982a, p. 23) emphasize that identifying no negative employment impact does not imply that there would be no welfare costs.

The question which of the aforementioned models represents best the way labor markets operate is highly debated among economists. Card and Krueger (1997, p. 383) for example prefer models in which companies set wages (e.g. monopsony or monopsonistic competition) instead of the neoclassical and its related models which all share the assumption that firms take wages as given which is according to the authors unrealistic especially when considering the low wage market. Ghellab (1998, p. 8) on the other hand points out, that the models mentioned by Card and Krueger indeed suggest a link between MWs and no negative or even positive employment effects but emphasizes that it would not be reasonable to assume that this link must always hold true. Other authors even admit that monopsonistic situations exist but also point out that this is rarely the case and consider perfect competition and therefore the neoclassical model as a tolerable approximation to reality (Dolado et al., 1996, p. 330).

Based on Germany, the central question is whether the domestic labor market is better characterized by the neoclassical or the monopsony model, which can hardly be answered in a general format. Bachmann et al. (2008, p. 15) explain for instance that there are various labor market constellations in different regions and industries as well as for workers with diverse educational qualifications.

In summary, it can be stated that disemployment effects prevail in the theoretical literature and are more likely to occur the higher the level of the MW is relative to employees' productivity, the less elastic the supply for labor, the more elastic the demand and the smaller the investment reactions of workers and firms (OECD, 1998, p. 42). According to many economists such as Schmidt (2008, p. 21) the appearance of these negative employment effects is just a matter of time because companies would substitute labor with capital or even offshore manufacturing plants if workers' productivity would fall behind the wage rate. As already mentioned young and low-skilled individuals are especially affected by these disemployment effects, which have enduring negative consequences for their future careers, as well as for the entire economy which will be shown in the following sections.

Table 1: The Effect of the MW in different Models

	Predicted Effect of MW on Employment		Predicted Effect on Wages		Predicted Effect of MW on Firm Profits	Main Point of Criticism
	Covered Workers	Uncovered or Higher-Wage Workers	Covered Workers	Uncovered or Higher-Wage Workers		
2.1.2 Neoclassical Model	negative	–	positive	–	negative	unrealistic assumptions (e.g. perfect competition)
2.1.3 Monopsony Model	positive (negative only if MW>W*)	–	positive	–	negative	hard to observe in reality
2.1.4 Oligopsony and Monopsonistic Competition	positive or negative	–	positive	–	negative	effects hard to predict
2.1.5 Two-Sector Model	negative or ?	positive (negative for the unproductive sector)	positive	negative	negative: CS positive: US	unrealistic assumptions (e.g. homogenous workers)

2.1 The Theory of Minimum Wages

	Predicted Effect of MW on Employment		Predicted Effect of MW on Wages		Predicted Effect of MW on Firm Profits	Main Point of Criticism
	Covered Workers	Uncovered or Higher-Wage Workers	Covered Workers	Uncovered or Higher-Wage Workers		
2.1.6 Heterogeneous Workers	negative	positive or negative	positive	positive	negative	wages increase for all workers
2.1.7 Efficiency Wage Model	—	positive	positive (potentially negative in long run)	—	positive or ?	limited empirical evidence
2.1.8 Lagged Adjustment	short run: ? long run: negative	—	positive	—	negative	"leads" are also possible

(Source: Own illustration; ?: effect is unclear)

2.2 Youth Labor Markets and Youth Unemployment

During recent times the global economic crisis has hit youth hard. Young people seeking employment are finding it very difficult to remain competitive, which is because school-leavers are facing increasing competition from experienced job seekers for fewer vacancies, and meanwhile employers can afford to be quite selective in their hiring of new employees (Scarpetta et al., 2010, p. 9). As a result the youth unemployment rate in the EU28 reached a historic high of 22.8% in September 2012 (2007: 15.7%), affecting around 5.5 million young people (Eurofund, 2012, p. 4). Table 2 shows among other data the unemployment rates for those aged 15-24 in the countries which are selected in the later review. The numbers vary considerable between the countries with rates ranging from 8% in Germany to 56.9% in Greece. Furthermore long-term youth unemployment[5] has risen strongly since 2008. While the share of long-run joblessness of youth unemployment reached a level of 22.8% in 2008, it increased substantially up to an average of 30% in 2011 (Eurofund, 2012, p. 8).

Due to these dramatic developments, several economists and organizations are already talking about a "lost generation" implying huge negative consequences not only for the affected individuals but also for the national economy (Eichhorst et al., 2013, p. 7; Dietrich, 2012, p. 3). On the other hand, the European Economic Advisory Group (EEAG, 2013, p. 74) emphasized that the youth unemployment problem looks worse that it really is, as only a small share of the population of those aged 15-24 is actually in the labor force. Nevertheless, it has to be stated that the unemployment rates among young persons in Europe are exceedingly high and this is associated with a long list of negative consequences. This sub-chapter deals with these kinds of consequences and explains additional factors other than those from MWs that could influence the youth labor market. Before that, section 2.2.1 gives a short definition of the term "youth unemployment" and characterizes labor markets for young people in general.

---

[5]Long-term unemployment is typically defined as being unemployed for more than twelve months in a row.

Table 2: Youth (Un)Employment Rates and NEET Rates in Selected Countries

	2002			2012			
	Youth Un-employment Rate	NEET Rate	Youth Employment Rate	Youth Un-employment Rate	NEET Rate	Youth Employment Rate	Long-Term Youth Un-employment Rate
EU27	18.1	13.0	36.7	22.9	13.2	32.9	30.0
Belgium	18.2	16.1	29.4	20.3	12.3	25.3	31.0
France	17.4	10.3	29.9	25.0	12.2	28.8	29.0
Germany	10.1	8.4	45.7	8.0	7.7	46.6	24.0
Greece	26.6	15.3	26.5	56.9	20.3	13.1	42.0
Netherlands	5.6	4.0	70.0	9.5	4.3	63.3	13.0
Portugal	14.9	10.6	42.2	39.7	14.1	23.6	28.0
Spain	22.4	12.6	34.0	54.3	18.8	18.2	32.0
UK	12.0	11.1	56.2	20.4	14.3	46.9	25.0
US	11.9	12.1*	–	16.2	14.8*	–	–

All numbers given in %; NEET: 15-24 year olds not in employment, education or training
* Numbers from 2007 and 2011
(Source: Data from Eurostat (2013a, 2013b, 2013c) and OECD, 2012)

2.2.1 Definition of the Terms

According to Martin (2009, p.3) "youth" is generally defined as the time span from the age when mandatory schooling ends until age 24. For most countries, that implies the period starting with 15 years onwards. Within this paper the category of "youths" or "young people" is defined as those aged 15 to 24 years, as this definition corresponds with both national and European definitions of youth, for example in labor law (Dietrich, 2012, p. 10). Following the definition from the International Labour Organization (ILO), "youth unemployment" comprises all persons 15-24 years old who are out of work but are currently available for work, could start within the next two weeks and have looked for work in the past month. Therefore the youth unemployment rate is calculated as the percentage of young persons unemployed in the youth labor force (Dietrich, 2012, p. 11).

The described definition was criticized by Eurofund (2012, p. 1) since the youth unemployment rate does not adequately capture the situation of young people because those who are students or apprentices are also classified as being out of the labor force. For this reason the standard youth unemployment rate is typically calculated above its actual figure (Eichhorst et al., 2013, p. 3).

Consequentially economists and EU policymakers are increasingly using the concept of NEET (not in employment, education or training). As the abbreviation already implies, NEETs are those who currently do not have a job, are not enrolled in training or are not classified as a student. NEETs are therefore one of the most problematic groups in the context of youth unemployment as they are seen as disengaged from the labor market and perhaps also from society in general (Eurofund, 2012, p. 1). Eichhorst et al. (2013, pp. 5-6) assess this concept as a more informative way of judging the current youth unemployment problem in the EU and in calculating youth unemployment rates. However, this thesis uses both concepts since data for NEET rates are not always given.

Looking at the youth labor market reveals that younger people tend to experience periods of joblessness more frequently than adults as they are not settled into a defined profession and are more mobile than adult employees (Eurofund, 2012, p. 8). Therefore unemployment rates for youth are consistently higher than unemployment rates for adult workers and unemployment rates for teenagers (15-19) are even higher than those for 20- to 24-year-olds (Martin, 2009, p. 5). Typically jobs for young people in the EU can be found in retail, manufacturing and in hospitality. Some of these sectors involve a high share of part-time work which is why they are so relevant for youth employment because many young people for example decide to work part-time while they are studying (Eurofund, 2012, p. 14). Additionally, many youth jobs are only temporary but can be seen as a stepping stone to a permanent contract. On the other hand those working for a limited period of time are also those who are most likely to be the first dismissed in times of crises. Europe-wide these kinds of contracts rose considerably, leading to a share of young people in temporary employment of 42% in 2010 (Scarpetta et al., 2010, p. 17).

2.2.2 Factors Influencing Youth Unemployment

As seen in chapter 2.1, MWs which are set too high can lead under certain circumstances to an increase in (youth) unemployment. This section focuses on other factors apart from the MW which can influence the youth labor market and thus youth unemployment. These influential factors can be distinguished by the macro and the micro level. The first one deals with the characteristics of youths and youth labor markets as a whole, while the second level concentrates on the characteristics of individuals which affect their chances of finding employment.

Macro Level

The most important determinant of youth unemployment is the business cycle which has a substantial impact on the employment prospects of young people (Lovell, 1972, p. 420). In general the youth unemployment rate responds disproportionately to changes in overall unemployment and is therefore more sensitive to the strength of the economy than adult unemployment (Blanchflower and Freeman, 2000, pp. 54-55). A survey in the US conducted by Freeman and Wise (1982, p. 8) shows that when the adult employment rate decreases by 1%, the youth unemployment rate decreases on average by 2-5%. The reason for this sensitivity can be found by identifying the disproportionate presence of young people in certain cyclically-sensitive industries such as construction and due to their high concentration in temporary jobs (Scarpetta et al., 2010, p. 14). Those temporary contracts are more vulnerable to economic crises in contrast to permanent contracts since it is easier for companies not to prolong or enter into new temporary contracts than to lay off permanent employees (Dietrich, 2012, p. 28). Another important factor is the size of the youth labor force and thus the population growth rate in general. The more young people can be found in a labor market, the more jobs will be required to place them (O'Higgins, 1997, p. 34). The result of a survey conducted by Korenman and Neumark (1997) was that an increase in the relative size of the youth population of 10% will increase youth joblessness by around 5%.

Further influential factors are labor market institutions and youth labor market policies in general, the length and quality of the transition from school to work and the time of the year (Scarpetta et al., 2010, p. 19). According to Freeman and Wise (1982, p. 9) many youths are undertaking summer employment during their school or semester holidays, even those who are usually not working.

Micro Level

The most important determinant for youth unemployment on the micro level is the educational rank. Many authors emphasize that academic performance in school and university is positively related to both employment and wages after graduation and entry into the labor force (Freeman and Wise, 1982, p. 3; Scarpetta et al., 2010, p. 16). In OECD countries the difference between unemployment rates of young people with low levels of education relative to those with higher levels has tended to widen since the 1980s (O'Higgins, 1997, p. 47). So far, the lowest qualified group has suffered most from the current recession, meaning that young people who have only completed lower secondary education (early leavers from education and training) bear the highest risk of joblessness. This can be seen by the EU average youth unemployment rate in 2012 which reached 22.8% while it was 30.2% for low-skilled youth (Dietrich, 2012, p. 17).

Early work experience is another determinant of youth (un)employment. Freeman and Wise (1982, p. 12) found a very strong positive relationship between hours worked while in high school and later employment and wage rates in the United States. Young people who have already worked during school or their studies have also more experience in looking for a job and are therefore superior to those who have not worked before they enter the labor market (Martin, 2009, p. 5).

Further factors influencing unemployment can be found in the family backgrounds of young people. Dietrich (2012, p. 4) emphasizes that some youths tend to have fewer (financial) resources than others and in some countries a strong financial attachment to the family implies that they are less mobile and therefore geographically restricted within their search for vacancies. On the other hand, Martin (2009, p. 5) points out that young people with fewer financial obligations and stronger family support can typically afford to take short spells of unemployment less seriously. Furthermore, the ethical background might also play a role when looking for a job. Bell and Blanchflower (2010, p. 4) explain that minorities and immigrants are especially impacted by a drop in labor demand and state that black youths in the US have noticeable lower chances of working than white youths.

In conclusion it can be said that four factors are the most prominent determinants for the size of the youth unemployment rate. The first one is the business cycle which influences economic development and therefore the demand for labor. Secondly, the size of the youth cohort which affects the labor supply and thirdly the educational level of every single individual. Apart from these three factors, the majority of economists also highlight the importance of the relative wage level and thus the existence of binding MWs which were analyzed in section 2.1.

2.2.3 Consequences of Youth Unemployment

Almost all scientists agree that being unemployed at a young age has a long-lasting negative impact on individuals. For this reason many authors speak about permanent "scars" or "blemishes" which arise due to periods of unemployment in early years (e.g. Scarpetta et al., 2010, p. 16; Mroz and Savage, 2006, p. 292). This section deals with these long-lasting negative effects for the individual and shows what kind of costs might arise for the whole society due to youth joblessness.

Consequences of Youth Unemployment for the Individual

The most significant effect of youth unemployment is the negative impact on future wages. Unemployment experienced at a young age today will depress future earnings for several years or even for the whole career (e.g. Bertola et al., 2013, p. 86). Mroz and Savage (2006, p. 262) for instance discovered in their survey on the US labor market that a six month spell of unemployment at the age of 22 leads to 8% lower wages one year later and still 2-3% lower wages at the age of 30 compared to a situation with no joblessness in earlier years.

Besides the reduction of future wages, early unemployment also has a negative impact on future job prospects in general. During the 1980s many scientists thought that youth unemployment did not have long-term consequences on later employment (e.g. Freeman and Wise, 1982; Heckman and Borjas, 1980). This picture changed considerably. Today nearly all economists and associated scientists believe that youth unemployment leads to a significantly increased risk of future (long-term) unemployment (e.g. Manzoni and Mooi-Reci, 2011; Dietrich, 2012). Schmillen and Umkehrer (2013) estimate that for Germany one additional day of unemployment at a young age causes up to six days of additional joblessness throughout the later career.

The reason for the reduction in future wages and the risk of later unemployment can be found again in another effect of youth unemployment. According to O'Higgins (2009, p. 53) joblessness at a young age may permanently impair individual's human capital due to a deterioration of productive potential and general employment skills. Additionally, periods of unemployment at an early career stage are viewed by firms negatively and will be interpreted as lack of motivation and a sign for low productivity leading to worse chances for a future employment (Scarpetta et al., 2010, p. 16). Furthermore, early work experience allows youths to accumulate social competences and job know-how essential in later life and additionally provides an orientation for future career choices (Streissler, 2008, p. 35).

As the current situation depicts, low chances on the youth labor market in association with an economic crisis lead to avoidance strategies by young people. Those youths in the UK and especially those in the southern European countries are more likely to stay in full-time education or undertake further studies rather than to look for a job (Bell and Blanchflower, 2009). Other youths move to different areas or even other countries with better chances to find employment and with greater prosperity (Dietrich, 2012, p. 1). The rest alternatively stays at their parent's place and perceives this dependency on their parents as a social stigma (Schels, 2007, p. 6).

Moreover, unemployment at an early stage in one's professional career can negatively affect the emotional well-being of the individual. Joblessness leads to social exclusion, network losses and the disappearance of regular social activities (Schels, 2007, p. 11). This causes psychological damage and might have harmful effects to self-confidence, productive potential, happiness, self-esteem and health (Scarpetta,

2010, p. 16). A vicious circle is emerging as negative impacts on the emotional well-being of youths further discourages them from seeking work and make them "unemployable" (Croucher and White, 2011, p. 11).

The described negative psychological consequences can potentially lead to further risks. Being excluded from the labor market and social networks is associated with higher risks of drug abuse and antisocial behavior such as crime and political radicalization leading to additional costs for the society (e.g. O'Higgins, 1997, p. 53; Eichhorst et al., 2013, p. 1).

Consequences of Youth Unemployment for the Society

Most of the aforementioned impacts of youth unemployment lead to costs not only for the individual but also for the whole economy. These costs are wide ranging and to some degree purely hypothetical which makes the calculation of the total financial burden on a society very complex and difficult. To isolate the different types of expenses, many authors differentiate between three kinds of costs arising of youth unemployment:

1. Public finance costs (direct costs): e.g. unemployment benefits
2. Resource costs (indirect costs): e.g. unpaid taxes, unpaid social contributions
3. Other non-pecuniary costs (indirect costs): e.g. deterioration of human capital

While resource costs can be roughly estimated by comparing the income situation of an employed youth to that of a young person without a job, other non-pecuniary indirect costs are purely hypothetical and cannot be measured directly (Eurofund, 2012, pp. 67-68).

A survey from the European Foundation for the Improvement of Living and Working Conditions (Eurofund, 2012) calculated the costs of NEETs in the EU in 2008 and in 2011. In their analysis they estimated that the loss of NEETs' missing labor market contribution for the 26 Member States' economies was approximately EUR 119.2 billion in 2008, corresponding to ca. 1% of the aggregated GDP of the 26 countries. These costs represent the expenses to the economy of not being able to re-engage youths into the labor market. Furthermore, their analysis showed that resource costs (EUR 111.3 billion) were much higher than public finance costs (EUR 8.8 billion). For 2011 the results from Eurofund were even higher due to the recession and the large increase of NEET rates within most of the European countries. The organization calculated a rise of the economic loss in Europe of almost 28%, corresponding to EUR 153 billion (Eurofund, 2012). Table 3 highlights the findings from Eurofund's analysis and shows the total costs for those countries which are in the centre of our later analysis.

Table 3: Cost of NEETs in Selected Countries in 2008 and 2011

	2008			2011				
	Number of NEETs in 1000	Total Cost in € bn	% of GDP	Unit Public Finance Cost in €	Unit Resource Cost in €	Number of NEETs in 1000	Total Cost in € bn	% of GDP
EU26	11,988	119.2	0.96	9,894	757	14,146	153.0	1.21
Belgium	203	4.1	1.17	18,387	3,851	233	5.2	1.42
France	1,487	17.7	0.92	11,657	1,091	1,740	22.2	1.11
Germany	1,212	16.4	0.66	12,382	2,090	1,067	15.5	0.60
Greece	416	4.0	1.74	10,888	84	645	7.1	3.28
Netherlands	149	3.0	0.52	20,851	1,429	179	4.0	0.66
Portugal	265	2.1	1.24	8,136	474	313	2.7	1.57
Spain	1,029	10.8	0.99	10,400	975	1,379	15.7	1.47
UK	1,067	13.4	0.75	13,520	1,006	1,259	18.3	1.05

(Source: Adapted from Eurofund, 2012, p. 76 and p. 79)

According to Eurofund (2012, pp. 80-81), their estimations have to be interpreted as very conservative since the calculated costs did not address non-pecuniary costs of youth unemployment. On the other hand, the authors of the survey also admit that their hypothetical scenario was unrealistic because not all NEETs can be re-engaged in the labor force, meaning that Europe will not be able to save the complete EUR 153 billion.

Nevertheless, it can be stated that the consequences of youth unemployment are not only harmful and costly for the affected individual but also for the whole society. This is particularly the case if youth unemployment rates are high like those in the EU at the moment, where the effects are likely to be long-lasting. This is why some scientists are already talking about a "lost generation" or a "lost decade" which will be trapped in long-term unemployment (Eichhorst et al., 2013, p. 7; Dietrich, 2012, p. 3). Eurofund (2012, p. 83) additionally emphasizes the increasing risk of instability due to the large number of discouraged and depressed youths without jobs. According to them, first signs are already evident to some degree in violent demonstrations in Spain, the UK and in Greece.

3 European Evidence about Minimum Wage Impacts on Youths

Chapter 2.1 showed a slight dominance of theoretical models predicting disemployment effects of a MW introduction for the total labor force. This view was confirmed by the meta-analysis conducted by Neumark and Wascher (2006) who reviewed around 100 empirical studies which analyzed the employment impact of MWs in different countries which were published after 1990. The authors concluded that roughly 50% of the papers found negative effects on employment, while 40% came to no or insignificant results and only 10% detected a positive impact on the total labor force. After using more precise scientific criteria Neumark and Wascher achieved clearer results. According to them only 19 of these studies were left after they checked for robustness and external validity, of which only one out of 19 studies did not find adverse effects of a MW on the employment rate.

This chapter deals with the question of whether these results can be confirmed when studies are taken exclusively into consideration, which analyze the MW impact on the youth labor market. Before that, section 3.1 presents an overview of the various approaches, attempting to measure employment effects and then lists the strengths and weaknesses of these approaches. Furthermore it provides a short explanation of why certain countries were selected.

3.1 Measurement Methods and Principles of the Literature Review

3.1.1 Strengths and Weaknesses of different Measurement Methods

To assess the impact of MWs on the youth labor market, it is first important to gain a rough understanding about the importance of the MW in the wage determination process. Therefore it is not very useful to compare real levels of MWs from different nations because countries can vary quite substantially in their productivity levels or in their purchasing powers. Comparing relative levels of MWs is more appropriate and there are basically three ways to do this.

The first possibility is to convert the MW into purchasing power parity (PPP) measured in US dollars. This is used to determine the relative value and thus helps to avoid misleading international comparisons that can arise with the use of market exchange rates (Schulten, 2012, p. 128). Another common measure is to estimate the proportion of the youth labor force that earns the minimum. Unfortunately this becomes complicated due to the existence of many different minima within one country and additionally due to often missing statistics about the hourly wage rates of teenagers and young persons (Rycx and Kampelmann, 2012, p. 7).

The third and most widely used measure to evaluate the importance of the MW is the Kaitz index which compares MWs across countries relative to the national median or average earnings. A high Kaitz index indicates a relative high value of the MW and suggests that a large fraction of the labor force is affected by it (Rycx and Kampelmann, 2012, p. 7). However, the index also contains some weaknesses which is why analyses should not rely exclusively on this type of measure. For example a rise in the MW will affect the average wage and thus mitigate the impact on the Kaitz index. Therefore it is better to calculate the index relative to median earnings which are less likely be affected by increases in the MW. Finally, Kaitz indices might misrepresent the effect of MWs in nations where other institutions (e.g. collective bargaining or benefit systems) provide additional and higher wage floors which affect only some sectors (Dolado et al., 1996, pp. 324-325).

After evaluating the relative value of the MW, many different approaches can be used to assess the impact of the wage floor on youth employment. This section explains the five most commonly used methods.

Time-Series Approach

Studies using the time-series approach try to examine the MW effect on the labor market for young persons over time. Therefore the youth employment ratio is regressed against the Kaitz index and a set of other control variables. The reliability of results of this approach depend on the number of observations (length of the time-series), the covered period and the way in which different shocks (e.g. boom and recession periods) have been controlled in the model's specification (Ghellab, 1998, p. 12). Advantages are the simple interpretation of the results and the fact that short-term and long-term responses can be distinguished, at least in theory (OECD, 1998, p. 46). However, according to Dolado et al. (1996, p. 331), this concept fails to recognize the endogeneity of the MW since it is likely that a wage floor is increased faster when the economic situation is favorable. Furthermore, it is very hard to control fully for other supply and demand factors that affect employment. These omitted factors will be integrated in the Kaitz index because its denominator is the median or average wage which will be affected by demand and supply shocks. Due to this weaknesses Cahuc and Zylberberg (2004, p. 730) conclude that typically too many variables are left out in these type of studies so that conclusions reached by this approach cannot be trusted.

Cross-Section Approach or Longitudinal Data

In contrast to time-series studies which try to assess how youth employment would react over time to MW hikes, the cross-section approach compares areas which vary in terms of their importance regarding the MW. These areas can be different states, regions or sectors while the dependent variable is again either the youth employment or unemployment rate (Ghellab, 1998, p. 14). Studies based on this approach provide usually more reliable estimations as they can allow for greater variation in relative MWs across regions, industries or individuals. Disadvantages are the endogeneity problem which also applies to this approach and the fact that many of these studies capture only short-run effects (OECD, 1998, p. 46). Nevertheless, Cahuc and Zylberberg (2004, p. 731) emphasize that studies grounded in longitudinal data analyze the effects of MWs with greater precision than surveys using the time-series approach.

Meyer-Wise Approach

The approach was first introduced by Meyer and Wise (1982) who estimated how the earnings distribution would look like in the absence of the MW based on the distribution of earnings above the legal MW. Following this, the impact of the minimum on employment can then be inferred by taking the gap between the calculated number of employees with below minimum earnings and the actual number of workers above or at the MW (OECD, 1998, p. 46). Müller (2012, p. 20) criticizes this approach for solely relying on the neoclassical model which biases those studies using this approach inevitable towards negative employment results. The only advantage according to Müller is the approach's simplicity and its lower data requirements. Dolado et al. (1996, p. 332) add that a further weakness of this approach is that the results appear very sensitive to precise assumptions made about the distribution of earnings.

Mincer Approach

Jacob Mincer (1976) was the first economist who distinguished between MW impacts on employment and those on unemployment, depending on the active population reaction. The approach is therefore based on an employment-rate equation and on an activity-rate equation. Results of these two equations are matched which allows to indirectly infer the MW impact on youth unemployment (Ghellab, 1998, p. 25).

Natural-Experiment Approach[6]

The first authors who used this approach were Katz and Krueger (1992) as well as Card and Krueger (1994) who studied the impact of increases in the MW in New Jersey in 1992 and California in 1988, while Pennsylvania was used as a control group since it did not change the MW. Thus, the idea of the natural-experiment approach is to focus on two markets or areas, where one undergoes a big change in the MW while the other one does not and acts therefore as the control

---

[6]Studies using the cross-section approach or longitudinal data can also adopt the natural-experiment approach what can be often found in the empirical literature.

group. This control group should necessarily be similar in the way that it experiences same demand and supply shocks (Dolado et al., 1996, p. 370). According to Kluve and Schmidt (2007, p. 2) this approach is generally combined with the difference-in-differences approach since the employment situation between the affected and the non-affected group is compared (first difference) and will be analyzed before and after the change in the MW (second difference).

Despite the fact that this approach is often used in recent research, it also has its weaknesses. Ghellab (1998, pp. 16-17) for example claims that such an approach is specific to federal systems and cannot be easily adapted to countries like France or Spain where the wage floor is valid nationwide. Furthermore it is hard to maintain complete control over other factors, other than the change in MWs, which might trigger different employment effects between the affected group and the control group (OECD, 1998, p. 46). Finally, Bachmann et al. (2008, pp. 18-19) admit there is a high level of internal validity but identifies a lack of external validity as well as difficulties in the choice of the control group.

The primary aim of all the described approaches is to estimate the effect of an introduction or an increase of a MW on the (youth) employment rate. Therefore most of the studies which use these approaches interpret their results by calculating the elasticity of the labor demand:

$$Elasticity\ of\ Labor\ Demand\ =\ \frac{\%\ change\ in\ employment}{\%\ change\ in\ wage}$$

This elasticity shows the relative change in the (youth) employment level for a relative change in the (minimum) wage. An elasticity of labor demand of -0.5 for example implies that a raise in the MW level of 10% leads to a change in the youth employment rate of -5% (Danziger, 2007).

In summary, it can be stated that all of the aforementioned approaches have their strengths and weaknesses which is why Bachmann et al. (2008, p. 19) conclude that it would be necessary to make use of more than one of the measures. As we will see in the following sections, the empirical studies conducted so far have relied on different approaches, and have brought various findings, some of which have led to opposing conclusions, and thus Bachmann et al. (2008) claim that the results of studies are, to a certain extent, dependent on the choice of the measurement method.

3.1.2 Literature Review: Country Selection

Eight different countries were selected for this literature review and there are various arguments why they have been selected. As a start the eight countries can basically be divided into two main groups. The first group contains the UK and the USA which can be described as liberal market economies (LMEs) while the rest of the nations are generally seen as coordinated market economies (CMEs). LMEs typically allow for a much larger role to be played by markets in regulating the economy than in CMEs where the state or other institutions hold a strong coordinating position (Croucher and White, 2011, p. 6). Because Germany is characterized as a CME, it can hardly be compared with the US and the UK. Additionally, there are other quite substantial differences between both the US and UK, and Germany across other fields. For instance employment protection legislation is rather weak in LMEs which leads to more flexible labor markets (Raddatz and Wolf, 2007, p. 11). Furthermore labor unions are less powerful and the tax burden for low-wage workers is relatively low, in comparison with Germany and other CMEs (Franz et al., 2008, p. 10). Nevertheless, both countries are included in this review because studies from these nations are often cited by the proponents of a statutory MW in Germany. These surveys show surprisingly positive employment effects of MWs for adult employees, making them an interesting case in determining the reasons behind these positive impacts and whether this is also the case for the youth labor market.

The southern European states Spain, Portugal and Greece are selected because of their huge youth unemployment rates, ranging currently from around 40% in Portugal to ca. 60% in Greece (Eurostat, 2013a) and due to their long histories of MW legislation. Additionally, Spain is chosen for the fact that the country's MW law does not include a specific sub-MW for young workers which is uncommon in Europe, but a policy that, so far, has not been planned or requested in Germany (Recio, 2006, p. 143).

Based on current election programs (e.g. SPD, 2013) many groups in Germany are in favor of a MW ranging around EUR 8.50 which would be one of the highest MWs in the EU. Belgium and the Netherlands have MWs with a similar level and possess additionally an institutional framework which is comparable to the German one (Schulten, 2013). However, the main reason for analyzing the Netherlands is the fact that they have one of the lowest youth unemployment rates in Europe despite their high MW rate. Belgium on the other hand faces a relatively high youth unemployment rate but more interestingly its MW system is comparable to the German system of collective bargaining (Schulten, 2006, p. 75).

Despite the similarities to the other selected countries, many economists claim that Germany would have the highest congruence with France because its labor market institutions, its tax structure and its high level of employment protection are comparable with the situation in Germany (Fuest, 2008, p. 26). Furthermore France has one of the most stringent legal MW systems in the world and has experienced a very active MW policy in recent years which is why it can be taken as an illustrative example for the consequences of a strong MW (Gautié, 2010, p. 179).

3.1.3 Principles and Methods of the Literature Review

The studies for the literature review had to be selected from a wide range of research. Papers which explicitly mentioned young workers in their titles were always included but also studies which focused on the effects of MWs on the labor market in general were reviewed because some of them analyzed the consequences on the youth labor market separately. This was particularly important for countries where only a few papers have dealt with the employment impacts of MWs. Despite that it was problematic to find studies published in the English language for some of the smaller countries. In cases where not enough English papers were found, the problem was solved by using English literature reviews from other authors who summarized studies dealing with these countries. Nevertheless, at least for the US, the UK and for France a large body of research was found. Here the literature review tried to identify those papers which can be seen as most representative of a specific time period or a particular approach as not all papers could have been included in the review. In the following sections some of the selected studies will be presented in more detail for each country while a short summary of the most important results of each reviewed paper and for every single country is given in the appendix and can be found in Tables A.1-A.8.

Before the start of the literature review it is important to note that there exist substantial differences between the selected countries in the level of the MWs, the extent of differentiation and the ways they are set and operate, which can be seen in Table 4 and Table 5. Additionally the ways labor markets operate and the structure of their institutional framework are considerably different. Because of these differences the MW effects on youth employment for each nation should be examined for their own value and not be compared with each other. Nevertheless the different studies will give an impression of the impact of the MW on the job chances of young persons and show what kind of aspects play a crucial role in mitigating any possible negative effects of the MW.

Table 4: Key Facts about different Youth Labor Markets and Minimum Wage Systems

	BEL	FRA	GER	GRE	NED	POR	ESP	UK	US
End of compulsory education (age)	18	16	16	15	18	16	16	16	17
Age full MW usually applies	21	18	–	25	23	18	16	21	19
Youth Unemployment Rate (2012)	20.3%	25.0%	8.0%	56.9%	9.5%	39.7%	54.3%	20.4%	16.2%
NEET Rate (2012)	12.3%	12.2%	7.7%	20.3%	4.3%	14.1%	18.8%	14.3%	14.8%[1]
Long-Term Youth Unemployment Rate (2012)	31.0%	29.0%	24.0%	42.0%	13.0%	28.0%	32.0%	25.0%	–
Youth Employment Rate (2012)	25.3%	28.8%	46.6%	13.1%	63.3%	23.6%	18.2%	46.9%	–
15-19-year-olds in education (2008)	90.5%	91.1%	91.2%	86.8%	90.7%	81.7%	78.9%	75.7%	85.2%
20-24-year-olds in education (2008)	41.5%	45.3%	41.2%	48.5%	52.1%	36.5%	34.0%	29.3%	36.9%
MW in EUR (2013)	9.10	9.43	–	3.35	9.01	2.92	3.91	7.63	5.64
MW as % of median wage (2011)	0.50	0.60	–	0.51[2]	0.47	0.57	0.44	0.47	0.38

	BEL	FRA	GER	GRE	NED	POR	ESP	UK	US
MW as % of average wage (2011)	0.43	0.48	–	0.35	0.42	0.39	0.35	0.38	0.28
MW in USD PPP	9.46	10.17	–	5.35	9.25	3.83	4.55	8.24	7.10
Fraction of MW earners	11.4%[3]	16.3%[4]	–	15-20%[5]	4.0%[6]	6.3%[7]	3.8%[3]	1.4%[8]	1.3%[8]
Fraction of MW earners among youths	13.4%[9]	32.2%[4]	–	–	12.8%[6]	–	–	14.2%[7]	–

1: Number from 2011
2: This number was estimated before the huge decline in the MW rate in 2012
3: Ryx and Kampelmann (2012, pp. 7-11), 11.4% receive sectoral MWs
4: Gautié (2010, p. 156)
5: Number from 1987 (no other estimations available), Croucher and White (2011, p. 73)
6: Salverda et al. (2010, p. 305)
7: Number from 1994, Ghellab (1998, p. 31 and p. 61)
8: Siebert (2008, p. 20), UK: 1.4% of all full-time workers earn MW
9: Numbers for the Flanders region, Marx et al. (2009, p. 46)

Further sources: OECD (2010, p. 357), Croucher and White (2011, p. 23), OECD (2012, 2013a, 2013b), Eurostat (2013a, 2013b, 2013c), Schulten (2013)

Table 5: Youth MWs and MW Fixing Machinery by Country

	Sub Minimum Wage for Youths	Minimum Wage Fixing Machinery
Belgium	15: 64%, 16: 70%, 17: 76%, 18: 82%, 19: 88%, 20: 94%	negotiated by union and employers as part of national agreement, majority of labor force is covered by sectoral minima
France	16: 80%, 17: 90%	set by government on the basis of a formula foreseen in the law
Greece	15-18: 70% 19-25: 80%	set by national collective agreement between organizations of employers and employees
Netherlands	15: 30%, 16: 34.5%, 17: 39.5%, 18: 45.5%, 19: 52.5%, 20: 61.5%, 21: 72.5%, 22: 85% apprentices are excluded from MW	statutory MW (75% of workers are covered by sectoral wage bargains between employers and unions which also set MWs)
Portugal	<18: 75%, apprentices <25: 80%	statutory MW
Spain	none	set by government in consultation with trade unions and employer organizations
United Kingdom	16-17: 61.4%, 18-20: 83% (no fixed proportions)	MW set by the government after recommendations of Low Pay Commission

	Sub Minimum Wage for Youths	Minimum Wage Fixing Machinery
United States	16-18: 82.5%, students: 75%	passed by Congress and signed into law by the President at the national level, also conducted legislatively at the state level

Source: Neumark and Wascher (2010), Croucher and White (2011, p. 25), Schulten (2013)

3.2 France
3.2.1 Situation

The first nationwide MW in France was introduced in 1950. After a reform to the MW in the early 1970s, it came to be known as the SMIC ("Salaire Minimum Inter-professionnel de Croissance" – "interprofessional index-linked growth MW") and has risen since then in both real and relative terms (Gautié, 2010, p. 153). Among developed countries France has, according to Croucher and White (2011, p. 66), the most stringent and comprehensive statutory national MW mechanism.

In contrast to other countries, the relative value of the SMIC has tended to rise over the last 30 years; this is due to the two kinds of mechanisms that determine it. The first mechanism guarantees the index link to wage growth and inflation. This is achieved by the connection of the SMIC to blue-collar workers' basic hourly wage rate and by the link to the consumer price index (CPI). On the other hand, the second mechanism does not operate automatically like the first, instead it is discretionary. This means that each year, after consultation with the National Collective Bargaining Commission, the government has the opportunity to grant a higher increase than the one determined by the first mechanism by allowing for a boost known as "coup de pouce" (Gautié, 2010, pp. 154-155).

Due to these mechanisms the SMIC has reached EUR 9.43 in 2013 placing France behind Luxembourg as having the second highest MW in Europe. Additionally with USD 10.17 in purchasing power parity (PPP) it rates as the second highest in the world in relative values (Schulten, 2013, pp. 126-128). Furthermore, using the Kaitz index would also locate the SMIC as second worldwide. In 2012 the wage floor was 60.1% of the median wage rate and was therefore more than 20 percentage points higher than the US wage floor (Bertola et al., 2013, p. 81).

The SMIC is set at national level and covers all sectors except the public sector and a few other employment sectors which have their own MW. A sub-MW exists for 16- and 17-year-olds, who earn 80% or 90% of the SMIC (Ghellab, 1998, p. 54). Because of the high relative size of the SMIC and its broad coverage, the proportion of MW earners is quite large. Measuring the exact number of MW earners is difficult, thus only rough estimations exist. According to Gautié (2010, p. 156) 12.9% of all covered workers were paid at the SMIC level, while the proportion for the 15-24-year-olds reaches even 32.2%. One of the reasons for the difficulties in measuring the proportion of MW earners is the problem of unpaid overtime which is the most common way of circumventing the legal hourly SMIC, especially in the hotel or retail sector (Croucher and White, 2011, p. 67).

Many economists claim that the MW is to a certain extent responsible for the high youth unemployment rate in France and therefore also for the riots which occurred in some of the Parisian suburbs in 2005. To increase the employment rate of young people, many researchers demand a lower SMIC level particularly for the youngest workers (e.g. Ragnitz and Thum, 2008, p. 20; Schmidt, 2008, p. 22). In 2012 the youth unemployment rate reached its highest level (25%) in recent years, while it was even higher for young Moroccan and Algerian immigrants (Eurostat, 2013a; Mueller, 2008, p. 25). The question of whether the high SMIC level can be blamed for the persistently high youth unemployment rate is ongoing and highly debated. In 1994, a plan to adjust the SMIC and to lower the subminimum failed (Siebert, 2008, p. 20) but French employers and many economists still request the lowering of the SMIC levels for 15-24-year-olds (Schmid and Schulten, 2006, p. 122).

3.2.2 Effect on Young Workers' Employment

Many studies have analyzed the potential correlation between MWs and the high youth unemployment rate in France but since the year 2000 only a few empirical studies have been carried out. In summary it can be stated that the majority of the surveys found negative employment effects (Rosa, 1980; Martin, 1983; Fitoussi, 1994; Bazen and Skourias, 1997; Laroque and Salanié, 2000) while the rest concluded that the effects are statistically not significant (Bazen and Martin, 1991; Skourias, 1992; Benhayoun, 1993 and 1994; Skourias, 1995; Abowd et al., 2000). Some authors have further argued that the rise in the youth unemployment rate was caused by economic trends (Dolado et al., 1996) while others even came to contrary results in similar studies. Bruno and Cazes (1997) for instance found an insignificant positive impact of the SMIC on youth employment. One year later and after changing some of the specifications both authors (1998) detected insignificant negative consequences. The further section focuses on some of these studies while Table A.1 in the appendix lists all of the reviewed surveys, shows their results and summarizes major points of criticism.

Rosa (1980 cited by Ghellab, 1998, p. 24) was one of the first authors who investigated the impact of the SMIC on joblessness among young people. His panel study analyzed the period between 1963 and 1979 and found considerable negative consequences of the MW. According to the author the labor demand elasticity for young workers amounted to -0.41. This number implies that a 10% increase in the SMIC level would lead to a decline in youth employment of 4.1%. In a later study Rosa (1985 cited by Ghellab, 1998, p. 25) used a longer time series (1963-1984) and ended up with a slightly lower elasticity of -0.35.

Bazen and Martin (1991) criticized Rosa and further scholars for using the Mincer approach in their investigation. According to them (1991, p. 207), Mincer-type equations are not well based on the theory of factor demand except under some very restrictive assumptions. The authors mention that the Mincer approach is not able to take into account the impact of increases in the MW on earnings of other groups which compete with young workers. Due to theses weaknesses Bazen and Martin modified the so far used Mincer approach by using a disequilibrium wage adjustment equation and labor demand equations. Even though Bazen and Martin believed in a considerable disemployment effect, the authors estimated only insignificant youth MW elasticities in a range from -0.1 to -0.2.

Abowd et al. (1997) focused on the period from 1981 to 1989 because of the substantial rise of 10% in the SMIC level by the French government in 1981. In their paper they analyzed the relationship between one's position in the wage distribution and the likelihood of transition to a non-employment state (inactivity or unemployment). Abowd et al. concluded that young workers paid around the SMIC rate were more likely to become unemployed than those paid over the minimum. The authors estimated an elasticity of -0.25 for young men (20-30 years old), yet surprisingly found a lower elasticity for younger people (20-24: -0.12 (men), -0.125 (women)). Abowd and his colleagues explained this lower elasticity through employment promotion programs, which were mainly offered to younger people during this period.

In conclusion it can be said, that moderate disemployment effects of a MW can be found in France but they are difficult to detect (Sturn, 2008, p. 24). Neumark and Wascher (2007, p. 96) offer an explanation for this mixed evidence, arguing that a country specific combination of labor market institutions have made it less likely that MWs will have detectable impacts upon young workers' employment rate. In this context Schmid and Schulten (2006, p. 124) mention wage subsidies paid by the government as one of the reasons for the moderate disemployment effects for the youth labor market in the period 2000 to 2005. Despite the mixed evidence and the tendencies towards insignificant results, many economists like Siebert (2008, p. 20) still claim that the high SMIC level in France acts as a severe impediment to find employment, especially for low-qualified young workers.

3.3 Spain, Greece and Portugal

3.3.1 Situation

All three countries were hit hard by the current economic crisis and the accompanying decline in youth and adult employment rates. The Southern European states are furthermore similar in their relative MW levels and in their strong employment protection legislations, implying very rigid labor markets (Bertola, 2013, p. 80).

Spain

The Spanish MW "Salario Minimo Interprofesional" (SMI) was introduced in 1963 and started on a relatively low level. It is more relevant from a social policy perspective rather than from a wage policy perspective because it serves as a reference value for numerous socio-political benefits (Recio, 2006, p. 127). The SMI is set by the government in consultation with employer organizations as well as trade unions and its purpose is to protect employees by guaranteeing them a considerable purchasing power (Dolado et al., 1996, p. 347). Since the SMI was introduced its level has continuously decreased in relation to average salary (Croucher and White, 2011, p. 69). Today it reaches an amount of EUR 3.91 (Schulten, 2013, p. 127). This corresponds to 43.9% of the median wage of full-time workers (OECD, 2013b) which is one of the lowest values in the EU, and which explains why only 3.8% of the labor force get paid this minimum rate (Rycx and Kampelmann, 2012, p. 7). In 1998 the sub-MW for teenagers (15-19 years) was abolished after establishing a single statutory MW with no further distinction by age (Recio, 2006, p. 143). This triggered a debate about potential disemployment effects for young workers, which have been renewed in recent times due to the extreme rise in the youth unemployment rate. Currently, Spain has the second highest joblessness rate among young persons in the EU which has reached 54.3% at the end of 2012 (Eurostat, 2013a).

Greece

Greece was similarly devastated by the crisis and today has the highest youth unemployment rate in Europe. According to Eurostat (2013a) 56.9% of the 15-24-year-olds were without employment, whereas in 2009 this was only the case for 25.8% of them (Croucher and White, 2011, p. 72). Apart from the recession, many economists and politicians attribute these high rates, to a certain extent, on the existence of a relatively high MW which has discouraged the employment of young workers. Therefore the Greek government changed the MW legislation in 2010 and again in 2011, resulting in those aged 15 to 18 being paid only 70% of the national MW while young persons aged 19-25 receive 80% (Bertola et al., 2013, p. 91). Furthermore after exercising pressure towards Greece on behalf of the EU-Troika, the national government decided to cut down the nominal MW level by 22.8% at the beginning of February 2012. Due to this cutback the Greek MW decreased from EUR 4.34 in 2012 to a current amount of EUR 3.35. As a consequence of this, the Kaitz index, which was 0.51 in 2011, declined as well (Schulten, 2013).[7] After its introduction in 1953 and up until the start of the economic crisis, no concerns were raised by any political party about potential disemployment effects of the MW legislation, which is why only a few studies had been conducted analyzing the impact of the MW on the level of youth employment (Fotoniata and Moutos, 2010, p. 213).

Portugal

In Portugal the statutory MW "Salario Minimo Nacional" (SMN) was introduced in 1974 with the aim of improving the pay conditions for poorer employees and has been set by the national government (Ghellab, 1998, p. 30). According to Schulten (2013, p. 127) the SMN currently reaches an amount of EUR 2.92 corresponding to 57% of the median wage. One of the few estimates concerning the amount of workers receiving the SMW was published by the Portuguese Ministry of

---

[7]No updated estimations of the current Kaitz index for Greece have been published so far. Aside from that there is also no recent evidence concerning the number of workers employed at the minimum.

Labor in 1994 and states that 6.3% of the labor force earn the SMN (Ghellab, 1998, p. 31). After substantial increases in the period between 2008 and 2011, the EU and the IMF compelled the Portuguese government in 2012 not to increase the SMN level in the near future without their permission (Schulten, 2013, p. 129). The EU and IMF explained their decision also with the high youth unemployment rate which has reached 39.7% in 2012 (Eurostat, 2013a).

3.3.2 Effect on Young Workers' Employment

Spain

Table A.2 in the appendix shows an overview about the results of the Spanish studies. According to Croucher and White (2011, p. 70) methodologies preferred by the Neoclassical school were applied in most of the Spanish papers which explains in their opinion the critical view with respect to concrete government intervention in the labor market and related regulations.

A major problem in analyzing the impact of the SMI on the national economy is that the minimum has varied very little in relation to average earnings. However, in 1990 the change in youth rates produced a considerable increase in the MW for teenagers. Dolado et al. (1996, pp. 347-352) studied this 83%-boost for 16-year-olds and the 15%-rise for 17-year-olds. Therefore they compared the change in employment rates over the period 1990 to 1994 with the fraction of workers in the low-wage sector, coming to the conclusion that the increase in the SMI level reduced the youth employment rate (elasticity for teenage workers: -0.37) while the employment rate of slightly older workers went up. To take into account cyclical factors the authors estimated regressions controlling e.g. for the overall employment rate for adult workers and found similar results. According to them, companies substituted away from younger workers who had become relatively more expensive and instead hired older persons. In their conclusion the authors summarized their findings by stating that the rise in MWs in the early 1990s had reduced youth employment whereas the evidence suggests that the total employment rate even increased in this time period.

A more recent paper from Blazquez et al. (2009) examined the period from 2000 to 2008 focusing on the existing regional differences and the dynamic behavior of youth employment which appears to be particularly dependent on seasonality. Therefore the authors used static and dynamic models with a regional adjusted Kaitz index. In summary they concluded that increases of MWs have lagged effects on employment. Besides that they found no definitive evidence of any disemployment effects of the MW on young people in Spain within the analyzed period. They even detected positive effects when not considering the existing regional differences, the lags and the seasonal work variations and interpreting these results as evidence for the existence of a monopsonistic labor market. Nevertheless, the authors admit that their results can also be compatible with a perfect competitive market where structural changes and a dynamic factor in labor demand coexist together.

Greece

The only study directly addressing the subject of MW effects upon the Greek youth labor market was conducted by Karageorgiou (2004). Within this study the author uses various model specifications and time series techniques and concludes that young workers older than 19 years suffer from disemployment impacts due to the MW while for teenagers the effect of a MW increase is positive in most of the specifications. Precisely, the elasticity for youth employment ranges from +0.15 to -0.25 whereas the impact on teenage employment is estimated between -0.09 and +0.68. Even though the results are not significant, the author states that one effect of the single MW for all ages (valid until 2010) is that companies tended to substitute more expensive and skilled young workers by teenage employees because teenagers could be employed with a lower training wage.

Further insignificant results were found by Neumark and Wascher (2003a) who estimated the elasticity of youth employment to be about -0.1 and by Koutsogeorgopoulou (1994). The latter focused on the MW elasticity of workers of all ages in the manufacturing sector and found a weak correlation located between -0.05 and -0.11.

Portugal

Studies concerning the MW impact on the Portuguese youth labor market show overall weak, negative effects. Ribeiro (1993) for example carried out an empirical study in which she used a very classical equation similar to that used by Cousineau[8]. In this context she selected six

---

[8] A detailed description about the Cousineau approach can be found in Cousineau et al. (1992).

groups of workers: male and female teenagers, male and female young workers as well as male and female adult workers. The author summarized her results by concluding that the MW impact is higher on women's employment rate than on men's and higher on youth employment than on the employment rates for adults. In total she found modest disemployment effects on youth employment ranging between -0.1 and -0.2 with the only exception for women aged 20-24. For this group she estimated an elasticity of -0.474 and explains this with the fact that the proportion of MW earners is higher on average among this group of workers (Ribeiro, 1993, cited by Croucher and White, 2011, p. 31).

A more recent study was published by Pereira (2003) who analyzed a quasi-natural experiment which took place in Portugal in 1987. Starting on January the legal MW for workers aged 18 and 19 was raised to the full adult rate, implying a 49.3% increase for this age group. Pereira concluded that this shock was rather harmful for teenagers' employment since the elasticity was estimated between -0.2 and -0.4. Furthermore the author found evidence of lagged responses and of some substitution towards older workers because employment level of adults has risen slightly after the change in the MW law.

3.4 Belgium and the Netherlands

3.4.1 Situation

Belgium

The Belgian MW "Revenu Minimum Mensuel Moyen Garantie" (RMMMG, guaranteed average minimum monthly income) was introduced by a collective labor agreement in February 1975 (Schulten, 2006, p. 72). The system contains minima in different sectors which are established through decentralized collective bargaining as well as a binding MW that is defined at the national level. Nowadays, the majority of the labor force (ca. 90%) is covered by sectoral MWs rather than by the national minimum and Rycx and Kampelmann (2012, p. 7) estimate that 11.4% receive sectoral MWs. Adjusting the MW level can be achieved in two ways. Firstly, the MW is linked to the development of prices whereas the second possibility involves labor unions and employers who are entitled to increase the MW higher than the inflationary adjustment within biennial cross-sectoral negotiations (Schulten, 2006, p. 73). These two mechanisms have contributed to the fact that MW's purchasing power was kept stable since its introduction and has reached an amount of EUR 9.10 in 2013 which represents according to the OECD (2013b) 50.3% of the median wage. Special rates exist for young workers starting at 64% for 15-year-olds and going up to 94% of the MW for 20-year-olds (Schulten, 2006, p. 73). According to estimations conducted by Marx et al. (2009, p. 46) for the region of Flanders, 13.4% of young workers receive the RMMMG while further 16.9% get paid 10% more than the minimum. Despite the frequent incidence of MW earners among youths and the persistent high youth unemployment rate of over 20% (2013: 24.6%, Eurostat, 2013a), the MW was rarely a topic in the public debate over the past few years (Schulten, 2013, p. 128).

The Netherlands

The current system was introduced in 1968 and contains a number of special features. The first is the coupling of the MW to the minimum benefits of social insurance and social provisions which has led to a steep, policy-driven decrease in the purchasing power of the MW and its relative position in wage distribution (Salverda, 2010, p. 299). Nevertheless, in a European comparison the MW is still very high and reaches an amount of EUR 9.01 which represents 47.4% of the median wage (Schulten, 2013, pp. 127-130). The other unique feature of the Dutch MW system is the long tail of youth minima. Workers aged 15-22 are entitled to lower MWs, following an age-related classification ranging from 30% of the adult rate for 15-year-olds to 85% for 22-year-olds with a separate MW for each year of age (Salverda, 2010, p. 300). While trade unions are in favor of lowering the age for the adult rate to 18 or 21, some politicians are even supporting the increase of the youth MW to age 27 (Croucher and White, 2011, p. 86). According to Salverda (2010, p. 302) one of the reasons for the relatively low minimum for teenagers is the concern that higher earnings would make employment too attractive compared to continued schooling or studying which could lead to earlier school leaving rates and thus to an overall decline in worker's productivity. Despite these low youth MWs, Salverda (2010, p. 305) estimated that 12.8% of the 15 to 24-year-olds earn the minimum while the percentage of adult MW earners amounts to 2.4%. Only this small fraction is directly affected by the MW since the majority of the Dutch people (75% in 1996) are covered by sectoral wage negotiations between unions and employers (Dolado et al., 1996, p. 344). Due to the low youth MWs, the wage restraints and the increased competitiveness, the Netherlands has one of the lowest youth unemployment rates in the EU which amounted to 9.5% in 2012 (Eurostat, 2013a).

3.4.2 Effect on Young Workers' Employment

Belgium

So far no study in Belgium focused particularly on the impacts of a MW on the youth labor market since the research is dominated by studies about active welfare state policies and their effects on the unemployment trap. Cockx et al. (2004) for example analyzed whether the income-support policy for unemployed persons accepting to work part-time increases the transition from unemployment to non-subsidized "regular" employment. The authors conclude that this policy has only a significant positive effect on the transition to "regular" employment when unobserved heterogeneity was not controlled for. Thus, they interpret their results in the way that unemployment among less educated young women can be explained by a lack of demand rather than a lack of financial incentives.

A more recent study by van Hemel and Darquenne (2009) used a qualitative sociological perspective since they documented the strategies and experiences of young persons who are in the group of NEET through interviews. The results showed that social and psychological aspects are rather perceived as impediments in the transition from school to work as financial aspects (e.g. the MW). Non-financial aspects are various and a broad list was named by the interviewed youths. For example bad first experiences in the labor market as well as bad experiences in school which causes low motivation for the further process of job search and/or vocational training. From van Hemel's and Darquenne's point of view it would make more sense to allocate more resources to job coaching and to offer real choices instead of sanctioning unemployed young persons (van Hemel and Darquene, 2009, cited by Croucher and White, 2011, p. 79). Nevertheless, the Flemish employers' organization VOKA stated that the Belgian MW would be too high and therefore acts as a crucial impediment in the transition from school to work (Ballegeer and Duvillier, 2009, cited by Croucher and White, 2011, p. 79).

The Netherlands

Dutch studies about the impact on the MW on the youth labor market suffer some severe difficulties which makes detecting the effects on employment hard or even impossible. Ackerman and Klaasen (1998, cited by Croucher and White, 2011, p. 88) for example explain that the majority of the Dutch companies are not paying the new and lower MW rates for youths and only 6% of young employees receive a wage at these levels. Dolado et al. (1996, p. 344) add that 75% of all workers are covered by sectoral MWs which are typically higher than the legal minimum. This implies that the gap between the youth and the adult MW might not be as large as the legal minimum suggests. Furthermore, the authors emphasize that the link between the MW and unemployment benefits makes it difficult to disentangle the effects of benefit changes form MWs, even though these effects could be different.

These complications could be the reason why many Dutch studies have arrived at such ambiguous results. Van Soest (1994) for instance looked at the macro and micro evidence of the unemployment effects of the MW in the period between 1984 and 1987. The author found that long-term impacts of the minimum on the unemployment rate were lower for youths (elasticity: -0.31 to -0.36) than for adult workers (-0.37 to -0.56) while the micro-econometric analysis has led to different results. Here, the youth employment level was substantially affected by the MW with elasticities of -0.59 for young men and -0.54 for young women in 1984 and similarly significant results in 1987. Dolado et al. (1996, pp. 344-345) criticized van Soest's estimations because his methods used to identify the impact of MWs on employment are rather dubious because the assumptions are not justifiable and specification or robustness tests were not carried out. The group of authors criticized also the approach by Koning et al. (1995) who used an equilibrium search model and concluded that a 10% increase of the MW would raise structural unemployment among young people between 5.2% and 10.1%. Dolado et al. (1996, p. 345) note that Koning et al. ignore the large amount of research showing other possible reasons for an increase in unemployment and state that they focus solely on the MW as a constraint for youth employment.

On the other hand, Dolado et al. (1996) took a simpler approach by focusing on the biggest decline in the Dutch MW system in 1981 and 1983 where the fraction of the adult MW received by 20-year-olds decreased from 77.5% to 61.5% and from 47.5% to 34.5% for 16-year-olds.

The authors concluded that this cut in the youth minimum increased the employment of young workers relative to the overall economy in occupations most likely to be affected (e.g. agricultural and textile sector). Nevertheless, Dolado et al. (1996, pp. 346-347) admit that the differences between the analyzed sectors were on the margins of statistical significance and this is why they stated that evidence from the Netherlands about the disemployment effects of a MW is scarcely compelling. Salverda (2010, pp. 318-320) agrees with this opinion by describing that the MW would have no effect on employment but rather on the distribution of wages and earnings inequality and add that reducing the size of the MW has enabled the growth of low-wage employment in the Netherlands.

3.5 United Kingdom and the United States of America

3.5.1 Situation

United Kingdom

The British "National Minimum Wage" (NMW) was introduced in 1999. However, MWs have always played an important role in the United Kingdom and an industry-based system of MW floors has operated from 1909 to its abolition in 1993. The NMW is set by the government after annual recommendations given by the Low Pay Commission (LPC) which consists of academics and representatives of workers and employers (Machin et al., 2003, p. 157). Especially because of this independent group of experts, the NMW meets broad support by the public life as well as by all political parties. Companies for example regard it as very positive that changes of the minimum rate are published six months before implementation to ensure that appropriate adjustments can be undertaken on time (Burgess, 2006, p. 54). With EUR 7.63 the MW in the UK was the sixth largest in Europe but is relatively not very high and corresponds only to 48% of the median wage (Schulten, 2013). Indeed, the Low Pay Commission (2005, p. 27) estimated that this level was equivalent to 55% of the median wage in the northeast of the country but only to 35% in London, making a decent standard of living impossible. Minimum levels for youths are even lower, accounting for 61.4% of the adult NMW for 16-17-year-olds and 83% for young persons aged 18 to 20. In contrast to other countries these levels are not fixed proportions but have been set separately on recommendations by the LPC (Croucher and White, 2011, p. 25). The aim of the low youth MW levels was, according to Ghellab (1998, pp. 56-57), to maximize employment opportunities for young people. Even though MW rates for young workers are relatively low, high proportions of young people are earning youth minimum rates (38% of the 16-17-year-olds and 26% of the 18-20-year-olds, Low Pay Commission, 2010, pp. 126-127) while only 1.4% of adult workers receive the NMW (Siebert, 2008, p. 20). Despite the low MW levels for young employees, the UK faces also a relatively high youth unemployment rate of 20.4% (Eurostat, 2013a) which is why employers' associations claim that the youth NMW would be too high and should be reduced (Burgess, 2006, p. 53).

United States of America

In the US a national MW was introduced in 1938. Today MWs are determined at Federal and State levels with many states having their own MW laws. This development has increased in recent times and thus fourteen states already have minimum rates higher than the Federal MW of EUR 6.64. Compared to countries of the EU, the USA has one of the lowest relative minimum rates corresponding to 38% of the median wage (Schulten, 2013). Due to this small value only 1.3% of the labor force earn the Federal MW (Siebert, 2008, p. 20), which is the lowest proportion of all the analyzed countries. This low number can also be explained by the fact that in cases where a worker is subject to both the State and Federal MW laws, the person is entitled to the higher one of the two wage floors. Like other countries, the US has also lowered MWs for younger workers. While students receive 75% of the Federal minimum, teenagers aged 16 to 18 earn 82.5% (Croucher and White, 2011, pp. 25-26). Surprisingly, many employers do not pay this sub-MW but rather the full adult rate and explain this by stating that they would not attract enough skilled teenagers with this lower rate and furthermore perceive it as an unfair wage (Ghellab, 1998, pp. 53-54). Compared to Europe, the USA has a lower level of joblessness among youths. However, in 2012 the youth unemployment rate reached 16.2% (Eurostat, 2013a) and this is why the United States in 2009 launched youth programs funded by the Recovery Act with the aim of giving special support to young people not employed or in education (Scarpetta, 2010, p. 24).

3.5.2 Effect on Young Workers' Employment

United Kingdom[9]

There have been only a few studies in the United Kingdom dedicated to the effects of the NMW upon youth employment, some of them commissioned by the LPC. Most of the British surveys focused on the impact on the total labor force. One of these surveys is the study by Stewart (2002). In this paper the author employed three different datasets to estimate the impact of the introduction of the NMW in April 1999. Using a difference-in-differences estimator, Stewart analyzed the effects of the newly introduced MW on the probability of subsequent employment among those groups whose wages have been raised to comply with the minimum. He found that the employment growth in areas with high proportions of low-wage workers was not significantly lower compared to areas with lower proportions of MW earners. Nevertheless, he detected negative but insignificant employment effects for those aged 18-21.

The study was criticized by Neumark and Wascher (2006, p. 84) for looking only at a time period of one year after the MW introduction and therefore neglecting lagged effects. In response to this criticism Stewart (2004) reviewed his approach and set up a new study in which he studied a longer period as well as the subsequent increases of the MW in 2000 and 2001. Again, he found no adverse employment effects for young persons and only negative but statistically insignificant impacts for adult women.

The only study specifically analyzing the effect of the NMW on the labor market outcomes of young people was commissioned by the LPC and conducted by Dickens et al. (2010). The authors focused on young people a few months older or younger than 22 because those aged 22 receive a legislated markup of approximately 20% on their MW. Those above the threshold were considered as a treatment group while those just below were perceived as a control group. Dickens et al. found surprisingly significant positive effects on employment and stated that on

---

[9]See Table A.7 in the appendix for an overview of the British studies which analyze the MW impact on the youth labor market.

turning 22, the employment rate among low-skilled persons increases by around five percentage points. The authors explain this with higher motivation for labor market participation due to higher wages.

United States of America

Studies about the effects of a wage floor on the American youth labor market are numerous and therefore cannot all be summarized in this section. However, Table H in the appendix presents some of the most interesting papers, while this part focuses on three of these analyzed studies.

Prior to 1982 numerous studies on the MW impacts on the youth labor market had been conducted, which is why the Minimum Wage Study Commission of Congress saw the need to assess these surveys. Brown et al. (1982b) have been commissioned to review the existing body of research and divided the papers in two different approaches. The first set of papers contained thirteen time-series studies which were all conducted during the 1970s and found consistent negative employment effects for young persons, with the exception of one study which came to positive results. On average, the estimated labor demand elasticities laid in a range of -0.07 to -0.3, meaning that a 10% increase of the MW would lead to a reduction in youth employment by 1-3%. The other set of papers contained six cross-section studies which compared areas that differed in their MW level, contrary to time-series studies which assess how youth employment reacts over time after raises of the MW. Brown et al. found similar employment effects for this set of studies ranging from a 1-3% decrease in total youth employment. Williams and Mills (2001) criticized these initial estimates for being highly unstable because he perceived them as plagued by serial correlation problems and specification issues.[10]

Card and Krueger (1994) introduced a completely new approach for assessing the MW effects, called natural experiments evaluation. Therefore the authors observed the change in the MW in New Jersey in 1992, where the minimum rose from USD 4.25 to USD 5.05 while they compared the employment growth in fast-food restaurants in this state with the situation in Pennsylvania, where the MW was constant (USD 4.25). Additionally, they undertook a second comparison between high-wage restaurants and lower-wage restaurants which had to

---

[10] A detailed discussion of these problems can be found in Williams and Mills (2001).

raise their wage levels in order to comply with the new MW law. Card and Krueger's results showed no evidence for disemployment effects of the new minimum, especially for younger workers who are typically employed in fast-food restaurants. Furthermore they found that employment had increased at restaurants affected by the MW relative to high-wage restaurants. Card and Krueger's study was highly debated and many researchers followed their approach and conducted similar surveys. On the other hand, several economists also criticized this study. John Kennan (1995) for example stated that Card and Krueger's approach contained some weaknesses such as measurement problems and fragile conclusions. Neumark and Wascher (1993) pointed out that natural experiments first conducted by Katz and Krueger (1992) failed to consider lagged effects and thus lead to inflated positive results.

Nevertheless, a more recent paper from Neumark and Wascher (2003b) came to similar conclusions which pointed to positive effects of the MW on youth employment. Neumark and Wascher further examined the impacts of wage floors on skill acquisition and education and found negative effects on school enrollment rates which support findings of related studies with similar research purposes. In summary, Neumark and Wascher (2003b, p. 9) conclude that MWs reduce skill acquisition among young persons because it leads to earlier transition from school to employment and has additionally adverse impacts on on-the-job-training.

3.6 Discussion of the Results

Results from the literature review differ from country to country for various reasons. One of them is certainly the size of the relative MW, which shows large differences for the selected countries. These range from 38% of the median wage in the US to 60% of the median wage in France. Due to the relatively high value of the MW in France, many economists believe that it would have adverse effects on employment, especially for young or unskilled persons. In line with this argumentation, the majority of the reviewed French studies point to disemployment effects of the MW for teenagers and youths. Papers published in the 1980s or early 1990s found stronger adverse impacts than those studies conducted in the late 1990s which often show a weak, negative yet insignificant relationship.

Spanish studies confirm the French results and provide consistent evidence of negative employment effects for younger workers. Surveys covering Greece and Portugal are rather scarce and most do not specifically focus on the youth labor market. Nevertheless, the paper by Karageorgiu (2004) covered this issue and showed that adverse consequences would be higher for those aged 19 and above than for teenagers since the older workers are likely to be displaced by younger and less expensive employees. On the other hand, Portuguese studies indicate that increases of the MW for youths would have small negative impacts but more interestingly also reveal the existence of lagged effects and thus showed that changes in the MW can take up to two years before they take a noticeable effect.

Results from Belgian and Dutch authors are not very clear and hardly compelling. Reasons can be found in the fact that the Belgian literature focuses almost exclusively on active welfare state policies and their influence on long-term unemployment while studies covering the Netherlands are challenged with numerous difficulties in measuring the impact of MWs on youth employment. However, some Belgian surveys indicate that the MW could act as an impediment to young persons who are located in the transition process from school to work. Furthermore, Dutch evidence points out that MWs have reduced employment slightly in most low-paying sectors whereas some papers found rather insignificant outcomes.

In contrast to the above described countries, empirical results from the UK and the US lead to opposite results. Although literature directly addressing the MW impact on young persons' job prospects in the UK is rather limited, it can be seen that most of the papers indicate either insignificant negative effects or even positive impacts. The picture in the US is similar where a large body of research found predominantly no effects at all or of increased youth employment despite a raise in the MW. Apart from these employment effects, British and American studies also reveal adverse impacts of the MW on young people. Turner and Demiralp (2001) for instance concluded that the MW would reduce school enrollment among teenagers because they feel attracted by the higher wage and start working rather than continuing with school. The study was confirmed by many other economists who came to similar results and also found evidence for a prevalence of adverse effects of MWs for young employees on on-the-job-training (e.g. Acemoglu and Pischke, 1999). British literature concerning the impacts of MWs on the participation in education is not as numerous as those in the US, but also points in a similar direction. For example Frayne and Goodman (2004, p. 3) estimate that a raise in the MW tends to lead to a shift out of school and into the labor market, and also towards combining school and work. Nonetheless, the authors emphasize that the number of youths who will alter their behavior in this way as a result of increased wages does not appear to be significant.

In summary it can be stated that disemployment effects as a consequence of MW increases prevail, especially in those countries which can be characterized as coordinated market economies like France, the Netherlands or Spain. Liberal market economies like the USA and the United Kingdom show rather positive results which indicate that employment effects of a statutory minimum depend crucially on the labor market structure as well as on the relative level of the wage floor (Moser and Stähler, 2009).

4 Potential Impact of MWs on the Youth Labor Market in Germany

In June 2013 the German polling institute Infratest dimap conducted a public-opinion poll regarding the introduction of a legally binding MW in Germany. According to this survey 86% of the German population are in favor of a nationwide wage floor. The fraction of proponents has increased considerably in recent years and amounted already in 2006 to 57% (Infratest dimap, 2013). This chapter deals with the current situation in the youth labor market and tries to answer the question why so many Germans are in support of MWs and if there are already any sectoral wage floors existing. Afterwards, the chapter analyzes potential impacts of a statutory MW on the youth labor force. Finally, the chapter concludes with an overview of possible modifications within the system of MWs which might mitigate the adverse effects of wage floors on young workers.

4.1 Current Situation in Germany

4.1.1 Minimum Wages and Collective Agreements in Certain Sectors

Germany does not have a statutory wage floor; instead MWs are set by collective bargaining on a sector by sector basis (Bertola et al., 2013, p. 81). This tariff autonomy is guaranteed in the German constitution and can be found in Art. 9, Abs. 3. It ensures the right of the bargaining parties (labor unions and employers) to negotiate wages without state intervention and to determine them in collective agreements. In

2004 around 62,000 of these collective agreements existed in Germany, 34,000 of them were industry-wide multi-employer agreements and ca. 28,000 were company agreements. High variations in the agreed wages could be found in some sectors. For example in the bakery trade, monthly wages differed between EUR 974 in Saxony and EUR 1,306 in Bavaria (Raddatz and Wolf, 2007, p. 18).

During the last 20 years the high coverage of collective bargains in Germany declined from 70.0% of the total labor force in 1995 to 62.8% in 2007 (Bertola, 2013, p. 82). Most affected by this development are low-qualified employees and young workers who suffer from low rates of unionization (Schmidt, 2008, p. 21). The decreasing rates of coverage by collective agreements and the introduction of the Hartz reforms in 2003 contributed to the growth of the low-wage[11] sector in Germany.

The described developments triggered a debate concerning an introduction of a nationwide statutory MW but so far Germany has only MWs in specific sectors. The first sectoral MW was introduced in the construction sector in January 1997 and is valid for all domestic and foreign workers, as well as for all companies within this industry. Its legal basis can be found in the Arbeitnehmer-Entsendegesetz (AEntG) which was initiated due to an increasing amount of employees from foreign countries willing to work for much lower salaries than their German colleagues (Möschel, 2008, p. 29). Also covered by this law were the roofers sector, which were the first German sector to receive a unitary national MW in 2003 (Arctz et al., 2012, p. 2). The AEntG was further extended to letter services in 2008 and led to MWs between EUR 8.00 and EUR 9.80 for employees in this sector. According to Bachmann and Kluve (2008, p. 8) this was mainly done to protect the German Post AG from competition because their exclusive license was due to expire during this year, and rivals like PIN Group and TNT Post tried to enter the market by paying much lower wages than the German Post AG.

One of the newest sectoral wage floors is the MW for the hairdresser's branch which will be in force as of August 2015 and amounts to EUR 8.50 (Brautzsch and Schultz, 2013, p. 1). Furthermore, a few days before the German election the Federal Government gave the green light

---

[11] Low wages are officially defined as gross monthly wages which are below the margin of two-thirds of the median wage within one country (Kalina and Weinkopf, 2006, p. 97).

for another sectoral MW, which will apply for the stonemason industry (Bundesregierung, 2013). Due to the current decisions thirteen branches have their own MW and the German Federal Bureau of Statistics (2013) estimates that ca. 3.9 million workers are affected by these industry specific MWs, ranging between EUR 7.50 (security sector) and EUR 13.70 (construction sector in West Germany).

4.1.2 The Youth Labor Market and Youth Unemployment

While most of the European countries were hit hard by the recent debt crisis, it seems that Germany was barely affected. Between 2008 and 2012 unemployment increased in nearly all states in the EU, whereas Germany experienced a decline in aggregate unemployment from 7.5% to 5.5% during the same period (Bertola, 2013, p. 73). A similar trend can be found in the youth labor market. Together with Macedonia, Malta and Luxembourg, Germany is one of the few countries where the youth unemployment rate decreased between 2007 and 2010 (Dietrich, 2012, p. 12). Today Germany faces the lowest unemployment rate amongst young people throughout Europe at 7.7%, whilst the average of the EU amounts to 23.5% (Eurostat, 2013a). This is indeed more remarkable given the fact that the country has consistently had over 0.5 million unemployed youths since the 1990s and has suffered from a youth unemployment rate of more than 16% in 2005 (Schels, 2007, p. 5). According to Scarpetta et al. (2010, p. 11) Germany was already before the start of the economic crisis in 2008 the nation in the OECD area with the lowest youth/adult unemployment ratio (1.5) which can be seen in Figure 6.

Figure: 6: Comparison of Youth and Adult Unemployment Rate in OECD Area (2008)

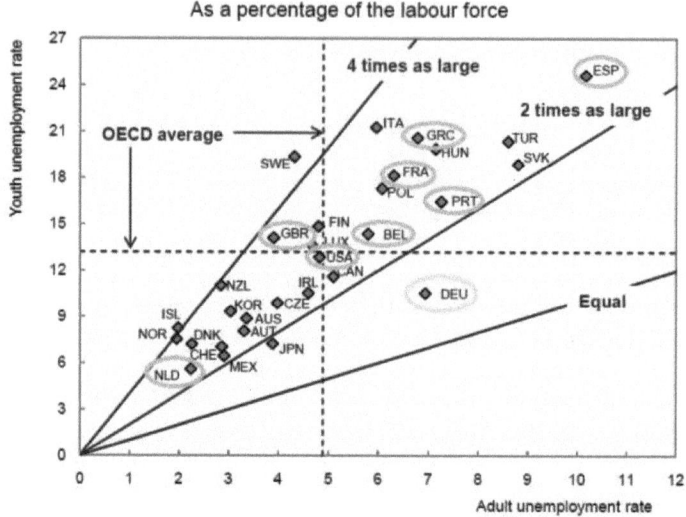

Source: Adapted from Scarpetta et al. (2010, p. 12), Germany (DEU) marked yellow; countries analyzed in chapter 3 marked orange.

In Germany only those persons without a job are defined as unemployed and who registered themselves at the national labor office, otherwise they will not show up in the official statistics (Dietrich, 2012, p. 11). For this reason it makes sense to consider the rate of young people not in employment, education or training (NEET) which was 7.7% in 2012 and thus also one of the lowest rates in the whole of Europe (Eurofund, 2012, p. 29).

Despite the very positive labor market statistics, some economists like Mueller (2008, p. 24) claim that young people in Germany have similar difficulties in making the transition from school to work and thus could hardly be affected by an introduction of a legal MW. The concerns of Mueller and other researchers are based on further labor market statistics. For instance almost 40% of the 15 to 24-year-olds are employed in atypical forms of employment like part-time work, fixed-term work or temporary employment (German Federal Bureau of Statistics, 2009, p. 12). This high proportion is also caused by large numbers of side and vacation jobs. However, Kalina and Weinkopf (2012, p. 8) estimate that more than 25% of the youth labor force is employed in fixed-term contracts and over 50% of them work in the low-wage sector. These numbers show indeed that young people are likely to be affected from the introduction of a legal MW.

4.1.3 State of Affairs in the German Minimum Wage Debate

For the past few years the potential introduction of a uniform MW has been highly debated. This section analyzes the causal reasons for this controversy; it presents the proponents and opponents of a legal MW and summarizes their main arguments.

Triggering Reasons for the Current Debate

As already mentioned in section 4.1.1 and 4.1.2, a number of factors have contributed to the weakening of the cemented wage structure in Germany. One of these factors is the accession of Central and Eastern European states into the inner-European market which increased the low-wage competition on the German labor market (Knabe and Schöb, 2008, p. 1). Furthermore, the Hartz reforms induced a wage moderation, which was achieved by raising the willingness of the unemployed with the help of various measures to take up low-paid jobs (Bertola et al., 2013, p. 78). The third major factor is the declining bargaining power of the different labor unions. According to Neumann (2008, p. 16) the unionization rate has decreased by more than 10% and Knabe and Schöb (2008, p. 1) add that the German trade union federation (DGB) lost almost 50% of its members between 1991 and 2007.

Due to these reasons, inequality at the bottom of the wage distribution strongly increased (Müller and Steiner, 2008a, p. 6). This can be seen by the expanding share of low-wage employment, which increased from 14.4% in 1995 to 23.1% in 2010 and is thus one of the highest rates in the OECD area (Kalina and Weinkopf, 2012). The increasing inequality in Germany is further expressed in the Gini coefficient, which rose during the last decade from 0.25 to 0.30 (Rürup and Heilmann, 2012, p. 340). These developments have contributed to an increasing fear amongst the population towards a downward sloping wage spiral that looks set to continue over the coming years (Sinn, 2008, p. 60).

Arguments of the Proponents of a Statutory Minimum Wage

The developments described above intensified the will of various groups[12] to implement a statutory MW in Germany. Basically their two main arguments are that "excessive" downward wage flexibility is no longer prevented by the existing wage bargaining system and that earnings of full-time workers should be generally sufficient to cover at least the means tested social minimum. Thus the defined goal of a legally binding MW would be to increase incomes of workers in industries with low union coverage and a large share of low-wage jobs (Müller and Steiner, 2008a, pp. 6-7). In this context the German trade union federation (DGB) is promoting a wage floor of EUR 8.50 in recent years with the slogan "Poor despite work. Germany needs the minimum wage." (DGB, 2013). Additionally the Social Democratic Party (SPD), as well as the Green Party, declared in their election programs to combat in-work poverty by introducing a MW in the range of EUR 8.50 (SPD, 2013; Bündnis 90/Die Grünen, 2013) while the Left Party even demanded a MW of EUR 10.00 (Die Linke, 2013).

Besides this, proponents of a legally binding MW often emphasize that a wage floor would be necessary to prevent companies misusing additional payments to low wages by public transfers, which, according to them, is often done in certain sectors. Furthermore, they argue that no conclusive empirical evidence for negative employment effects would result from this, but rather that some countries in Europe have received positive experiences with a statutory MW (Fuest, 2008, p. 26). Finally, some proponents claim a MW would raise the purchasing power of a country and thus mitigates its potential adverse effects (Sinn, 2008, p. 59).

Arguments of the Opponents of a Statutory Minimum Wage

The opponents of a statutory MW criticize the arguments of the proponents as highly naive which do not hold in the German context and which are based on misinterpreted international comparisons (Börsch-Supan, 2008, p. 38). Hans-Werner Sinn (2008, p. 57) claims a lack of objectivity within this debate, stating that most of the arguments of the proponents are based on emotions and feelings. This is why he assumes,

---

[12]An overview about the different proponents of a legal MW and their desired MW levels as well as a list of some of the opponents can be found in Table 6 after this section.

that the majority of the German population believes that a statutory MW is absolutely required from an ethical perspective. Sinn (2008) countered some of the arguments by declaring that the fear of a downward sloping wage spiral is clearly unfounded since the approaching situation of full employment would reverse this development. Additionally he claims that a MW will not increase the purchasing power of an economy because a wage increase can only redistribute the purchasing power instead of raising it. Other economists blame MWs for being protective measures with the aim of preventing competition by foreign workers and compare a potential wage floor therefore with illegal tariffs (Franz et al., 2008, p. 11). However, the major argument of the opponents is that a MW would increase unemployment substantially and the group most affected by this policy would be the group of young workers aged 15 to 24 (Mueller, 2008, p. 24).

Overview of Prospective Developments

In March 2013 the Federal Council of Germany voted for a statutory MW of EUR 8.50 with the aim to secure that all full-time employees receive a wage with which they can afford participating in cultural and social life. The German Federal Parliament had to decide about this bill in April and rejected it (Bundesrat, 2013). However, this happened when the Christian Democratic Union (CDU) and the Free Democratic Party (FDP) were holding the majority in the parliament. After the election in September 2013 this has changed as the FDP lost a high share of votes and is thus not represented in the new parliament. Today (status from 24.09.2013) the majority situation is rather uncertain which makes it difficult to assess the chances of an introduction of a legal MW in Germany. Nevertheless, it is quite likely that the SPD tries to push through their will of a nationwide MW in case of a grand coalition. In the rather unlikely case of a coalition between SPD, the Green Party and the Left Party a statutory MW of at least EUR 8.50 will be inaugurated with a high probability.

Table 6: Proponents and Opponents of a legally binding MW in Germany

Proponents of MWs in Germany	Opponents of MWs in Germany
Political parties:	*Political parties:*
Bündnis 90/Die Grünen (2013): EUR 8.50	CDU (2013)
Die Linke (2013): EUR 10.00	FDP (2013)
SPD (2013): EUR 8.50	*Employers' associations:*
Labor unions:	BDA (2013)
DGB (2013): EUR 8.50	*Economists:*
NGG (Initiative Mindestlohn, 2013): EUR 8.50	Börsch-Supan (2008): ex-chairman of the academic advisory council of the Federal Ministry of Economics and Technology (2004-2008)
Ver.di (Initiative Mindestlohn, 2013): EUR 8.50	Fuest (2008): president ZEW
Employers' associations:	Sinn (2008): president ifo Institut
ILS (2013): no concrete amount mentioned	Snower (Lechthaler&Snower, 2008): president IfW
Economists:	Straubhaar (2008): Managing Director HWWI
Güth&Kliemt (2008): MWs as help for coordination	*Others:*
Möller (Möller and König, 2008): different MWs	Council of Economic Experts (Franz et al., 2008)
Rürup (2008): EUR 4,50	Lagarde (Sinn, 2008): Managing Director of IMF
Others:	Trichet (Sinn, 2008): ex-chairman of ECB
86% of the population (Infratest dimap, 2013)	
Federal Council (Bundesrat, 2013): EUR 8.50	

Note: This list is not complete but rather a compilation of different groups and thoughts. Sources given in parentheses. Explanations for the abbreviations can be found below.

Proponents of MWs in Germany	Opponents of MWs in Germany
BDA: Confed. of German Employers' Associations	ECB: European Central Bank
HWWI: Hamburg Institute of Inter. Economics	ifo: Institute for Economic Research
IfW: Kiel Institute for the World Economy	IMF: International Monetary Fund
ILS: Association of Instore and Logistic Services	NGG: Food, Beverages and Catering Union
Ver.di: United Services Union	ZEW: Centre for European Economic Research

Source: Own compilation.

4.2 Simulation of Impacts of a potential Minimum Wage on the Youth Labor Market and Empirical Evidence from Germany

4.2.1 Empirical Evidence from German Simulations and Studies

Up until now, no German simulations or studies have analyzed the potential impacts of a statutory MW or a sectoral wage floor on youth employment in particular. Nevertheless, some results prove interesting because they contain answers concerning how many young people would be affected by this kind of policy. These findings will be briefly summarized in this section. However, all simulations and studies published so far cannot be outlined in greater detail. Therefore Table A.9 and Table A.10 in the appendix provide a description of the most relevant results of the reviewed papers and give a short overview of the applied approaches. Table A.9 contains information about conducted simulations while Table A.10 summarizes studies analyzing the impacts of sectoral MWs which can be found in some German industries.

Results from Simulations analyzing Impacts of a Statutory Minimum Wage

The first simulations concerning the impacts of a statutory MW in Germany were published in 2006, when the debate about in-work poverty and the demand for a legally binding MW slowly began. Today many similar simulations have been conducted, analyzing different kinds of consequences of a potential wage floor. Most of them focus on the question how many workers would be affected by such a policy or how large the employment effects would be, while others also analyze the impact on the purchasing power or on average wages. Some even try to estimate the fiscal consequences by looking at changes in the tax structure and in unemployment benefits (see Bachmann et al., 2008 or Bauer et al., 2009).

The majority of the simulations are based on data from the German Socio-Economic Panel (SOEP) and use estimated labor demand elasticities for different groups of workers as well as cross-price elasticities while other authors like Ragnitz and Thum (2007) or Knabe and Schöb (2008) assume constant elasticities.

Partly because of these differences in the data set and in the estimated elasticities, results differ considerably, especially for those assessing potential disemployment effects. These estimated employment losses of a MW of EUR 7.50 range from 161,400 (Müller and Steiner, 2008b) up to 1,189,000 (Bachmann et al., 2008). However, simulations finding large disemployment impacts prevail because four of the six estimations dealing with this question come to reductions in employment ranging between 0.8 and 1.2 million persons.

Results of simulations concerning the relevance of MWs for the labor force in Germany differ as well, but not substantially in contrast to those described above. Kalina and Weinkopf (2006) for example estimate that 64.3% of all low-wage workers and 45.0% of all persons with a side job as their main source of income would receive a MW of EUR 7.50. Youths are often represented in both of these groups which can be seen by Kalina and Weinkopf's estimation that 32.4% of all employed 15 to 24-year-olds earn less than the assumed MW of EUR 7.50. On the other hand Müller and Steiner (2008b) find a lower share of affected youths (22.4%), what can partly be explained by the fact that their definition of "youths" is slightly different (18-25 years). In another simulation, conducted by Knabe and Schöb (2008), the authors focused on different groups and estimated that 49.6% of all employed students (279,010 persons) would receive a wage rate of EUR 7.50 in case of the implementation of a MW. This result is in line with the findings of Brenke and Eichhorst (2007) who assume that 52% of this group earns less than EUR 8.00.

In more recent papers, researchers suppose a statutory MW of EUR 8.50 for their simulations because this level is currently demanded by many political parties and labor unions (see section 4.1.3). One of these papers is published by Brautzsch and Schultz (2013) who proceed on the assumption that 59.3% of all low-wage workers would be affected by a MW and thus earn less than EUR 8.50 at the moment. Again, this result is in line with a previous finding of Kalina and Weinkopf (2006) and shows that young workers are highly likely to be affected by a MW policy because many of them work in this sector. Furthermore a recent paper released by Brenke and Müller (2013) in September confirms this hypothesis by stating that 44% of all youths (18-24 years) earn less than the demanded MW rate of EUR 8.50 which is twelve percentage points higher than the estimation done by Kalina and Weinkopf (2006) and 22 percentage points larger than the simulation by Müller and Steiner (2008a).

Results from Studies analyzing Impacts of Sectoral Minimum Wages

The majority of the studies analyzing impacts of sector specific MWs use the natural experiment approach combined with the difference-in-differences technique, which ensures a high internal but rather low external validity (Kluve and Schmidt, 2007, pp. 2-5). Unfortunately, these studies do not focus in general on age related employment effects and are therefore not very useful to answer the question of how MWs affect the youth labor market. However, Müller's (2012) literature review regarding wage floor impacts on the main construction industry revealed large negative consequences for young workers (18-25 years) while the overall impact on the employment level is negligible. This view is confirmed by Aretz et al. (2012) who observed effects of the sectoral MW for the roofing industry. According to them, workers who receive the sector specific MW show a decreasing probability of continuing employment while employees earning above the MW profit from the change and have a higher probability of keeping their jobs. As seen above, those persons, who earn a MW because they got paid a lower wage before, are typically young and/or low-qualified. Furthermore studies referring to sectoral wage floors often come to the conclusion that workers in East Germany suffer more from a MW than people in the West, where some studies even detect positive employment effects (e.g. König and Möller, 2007). In summary Möller (2012), who compared many different studies which covered sector specific MWs, points out that disemployment effects based on sectoral wage floors can rarely be found.

4.2.2 Applied Method of the self-conducted Simulation

The purpose of the simulation is to estimate disemployment effects for young employees in Germany which might arise due to an introduction of a statutory MW. To calculate these effects, it is first necessary to analyze how many workers would be affected by a legally binding wage floor. In this context four different minimum levels are assumed: one low MW of EUR 5.00, which is demanded by Rürup (2008), one high MW of EUR 10.00 requested by the Left Party (Die Linke, 2013) and two medium high MWs of EUR 7.50 and EUR 8.50. As described in 4.1.3, the implementation of a MW of EUR 8.50 is currently the most likely minima level to be applied.

The simulation is based on data from the 2011 wave of the German Socio-Economic Panel (SOEP, 2011) which is also used by other simulations concerning the MW impact (e.g. Brenke and Müller, 2013). This data set is a longitudinal study of private households and their monthly income in Germany and contains ca. 29,000 individual observations. According to Knabe and Schöb (2008, p. 4) the sampling weights imply that these observations are representative for about 82 million persons. Observations of individuals with missing data concerning their gross monthly income or their amount of working time were excluded. For purposes of this simulation only young people between 18 and 24 years were considered as the data set does not contain information about persons younger than 18.

Furthermore data regarding hourly wages is also not given by the SOEP but can be calculated. Therefore, Brenke and Müller's (2013, p. 5) approach was used to estimate the hourly wages by dividing the gross monthly income by the product of weekly working hours and a constant factor of 4.3 (amount of weeks within one month). In accordance with the work of Knabe and Schöb (2008) all hourly wages below EUR 3.00 were excluded from further analysis. Müller (2009a) explains this with measurement errors at the bottom of the wage distribution. According to him, a comparison of the SOEP with a survey of the German Federal Statistical Office regarding the wage structure (Verdienst- und Strukturerhebung, (VSE)) showed that calculated hourly wages below EUR 3.00 in the SOEP are not very reliable. To gain a representative assessment of the group of young employees, the analyzed data set was weighted with the grossing-up factors of the SOEP.

Finally, to estimate how large the employment effects would be at different MW levels, the method of Knabe and Schöb (2008, p. 11) is employed. Thus, the simulation assumes a labor demand function of $L(w) = w\eta$, where w is the gross wage an employer has to pay for each worker and η is the constant wage elasticity of labor demand. Therefore, the employment impact of a wage increase from $w < MW$ to a new MW can then be calculated in the following way:

$$employment\ reduction(in\ \%) = \left(\frac{MW}{w}\right)^{\eta} - 1$$

The size of the elasticity rate used has a significant impact on the final results, which is why three different elasticity rates have been used. The first (-0.1) and the second elasticity (-0.3) are rather small but correspond to the results of chapter 3. Additionally, according to Neumark and Wascher (2010, p. 63), an elasticity of -0.3 seems to be the "best guess". On the other hand, Ragnitz and Thum (2007, p. 36) state that empirical estimates indicate a wage elasticity of labor demand of a magnitude of -0.75. This elasticity was also used in a study conducted by Bachmann et al. (2008) which is why this simulation considered an elasticity of -0.75 as a third scenario.

4.2.3 Results of the self-conducted Simulation

The analyzed data set contains 1,862 individuals between 18 and 24 years. Around 50% of them are currently in employment, which implies that the simulation is based on wage information from 918 young employees. In contrast to other German studies apprentices were also included because recent MW proposals (e.g. SPD, 2013) do not consider an exemption for apprentices in the case of an implementation of a statutory wage floor. Furthermore youths working part-time or having a side job were also incorporated, which is particularly important for the group of students. They usually belong to the older age group (20-24), which shows higher employment rates (55%) than the group of teenagers (33%). This can be explained by the fact that many of them are still in education.

Analyzing the current wage rates of young people in Germany reveals large differences between both age groups. Despite the fact that all observations with hourly wage rates lower than EUR 3.00 were excluded from the simulation, the group of teenagers contains almost 50% of employees working for less than EUR 5.00 while for the older age group this was only true for 19% which is indicated in Table 7. In contrast to Brenke and Müller (2013) the estimate shows a share of 56.9% of all young employees receive hourly payments less than EUR 8.50, whilst Brenke and Müller arrived at a 44% share of those who would be affected by a MW of this size. Furthermore the analysis reveals sizeable differences between various age groups, but also between male and female workers. The share of young women who would be affected by a MW is on average four percentage points higher than the ratio of male employees. Previously conducted studies confirm this view and come to similar results.

Table 7: Share of Young Workers who might be affected from a MW

	Share of young workers earning currently wages below a potential MW (in %)			
	below EUR 5.00	below EUR 7.50	below EUR 8.50	below EUR 10.00
Age				
18-19	47.47	77.78	81.82	87.88
20-24	18.93	43.53	52.91	69.09
Gender				
Male	20.95	46.42	54.91	69.76
Female	25.00	50.29	59.12	73.82
Total	22.87	48.26	56.90	71.69

Source: Own simulation based on data from SOEP (2011)

Looking at the disemployment effects indicate the importance of different MW levels and assumed labor demand elasticities on the later outcomes. Table 8 summarizes the findings and reveals that a low elasticity of -0.1 leads to moderate job losses for young workers, even in the case of a very high MW of EUR 10. The expected reductions in employment when considering an elastic labor demand of -0.75 are in line with the findings of other German simulations (e.g. Ragnitz and Thum, 2007) which assume the same elasticity in their studies.

Table 8: Disemployment Effects for Young Workers in case of different MWs

	Constant Elasticity of Labor Demand					
	−0.10		−0.30		−0.75	
	in %	number	in %	number	in %	number
MW of EUR 5.00						
18-19	−1.41	−7.840	−4.16	−23.192	−10.07	−56.184
20-24	−1.43	−39.407	−4.24	−116.534	−10.27	−282.130
Total	−1.43	−47.247	−4.22	−139.725	−10.22	−338.314
MW of EUR 8.50						
18-19	−5.09	−28.403	−14.51	−80.945	−32.43	−180.879
20-24	−3.76	−103.301	−10.86	−298.393	−24.99	−686.320
Total	−4.02	−131.704	−11.58	−379.338	−26.48	−867.199
MW of EUR 10.00						
18-19	−6.08	−33.917	−17.16	−95.689	−37.53	−209.342
20-24	−4.07	−111.865	−11.73	−322.114	−26.79	−735.865
Total	−4.39	−145.782	−12.61	−417.803	−28.61	−945.207

Source: Own simulation based on data from SOEP (2011)

4.2.4 Critical Assessment of the self-conducted Simulation

The disemployment effects found in the simulation above are far from being certain because they strongly rely on the assumption of a constant labor demand elasticity which cannot be found in reality. Despite the fact that the group of young workers is relatively homogenous when considering the age structure, this group does however show large variations in skill and educational levels. Furthermore not all youths are working in similar sectors with a similar elasticity of labor demand. For this reason further studies regarding the impacts of a MW on the job market for teenagers and young adults should consider various elasticities for different groups of young people. Müller (2009a, p. 19) confirms this view by claiming that approaches which take heterogeneous labor and substitution effects explicitly into account seem to be more fruitful. Nevertheless, the problem of applying constant elasticities can also be found in other German studies, which is heavily criticized (e.g. Fitzenberger, 2009).

Additionally the simulation above did not include the price elasticity of the demand for goods what is included in the study by Müller and Steiner (2008b). The reason for the relevance of this elasticity when considering MW effects, is the fact that a wage increase due to an implementation of a statutory MW, increases the price for labor which raises the costs for producing goods. A company who faces these cost increases will likely raise the prices of its products and thus affect the demand for goods, which again has consequences for the labor market (Kalina and Weinkopf, 2006).

Corresponding with other German simulations, my study also neglects the existence of spillover-effects and assumes that only the wages of workers who receive less than the MW are affected by an introduction of a nationwide wage floor. As seen in the empirical literature this cannot be true because wages higher than the MW can be increased by the employer to maintain the wage gap between low- and high-productive employees (Müller and Steiner, 2008b).

A weakness within the simulation is the fact that only the SOEP (2011) data set is used. Studies which consider two different data bases seem to be more successful in analyzing the real wage structure in Germany. According to Brenke and Müller (2013, p. 5) the SOEP underestimates the German wage level because it does not take into account special payments like the Christmas bonus or sales bonuses.

This underestimation leads to higher disemployment effects and thus biases the result.

Despite all its weaknesses, the simulation gives a first impression of the potential impacts of a MW on the youth labor market and reveals the importance of the MW level and the estimated elasticity for labor demand which affect the results substantially.

4.3 Modifications within the System of Minimum Wages[13]

4.3.1 Subminimum Wages for Young Workers

According to Croucher and White (2011, p. 92) adverse effects of MWs upon the youth labor market are more likely to occur when no separate subminimum rates for teenagers and young adults are set. This is also shown in the literature review which analyzed the effects in Spain where no sub-MW for young people exists (see section 3.3). The same was true for Greece, yet the government counteracted the increasing rates of youth unemployment by lowering the MW rates for 15 to 25-year-olds in 2011. Additionally, Bertola et al. (2013, p. 81) outline that Sweden is another example where too little differentiation by age increased youth unemployment. For these reasons the OECD (1994, p. 30) recommended members, in 1994, to sufficiently differentiate MW rates by age and if necessary also by regions.

Today sub-MWs for youths can be found in most of the OECD countries and in all of the eight reviewed countries apart from Spain. The success of those measures can be seen best in the Netherlands (see section 3.4) where the youth unemployment rate is one of the lowest in the EU. This is also achieved by the measure of granting young workers especially low MW rates. 15-year-olds for example receive only 30% of the adult MW while apprentices are excluded from MWs altogether (Schulten, 2006).

The purpose of assigning lower MWs for young workers is to stimulate the demand for low-skilled youths by reducing the cost of employing them (Scarpetta et al., 2010, p. 29). Furthermore low MWs

---

[13]This thesis is not dealing with alternatives to MWs like negative income taxes, wage subsidies or combination wages (Kombilöhne). An overview and critical assessment of these measures can be found for example in Shaviro (1997) or in Eichhorst (2006).

should reduce the supply of teenagers in the labor market by lowering the incentives to leave school early (Ghellab, 1998, p. 50). Based on this argumentation, the OECD (2012) currently recommends the complete exclusion of workers younger than 21 years from MWs, also in cases when the adult rate is set relatively low.

Subminimum wages have been criticized in the past by authors like Ghellab (1998, p. 48) who considered these measures as a form of discrimination towards young people because the principle of equal payment for work of equal value is violated when no formal training or apprenticeship has been provided by the employer. Therefore economists like Hicks (2010, p. 3) suggest the introduction of a tenure scaled MW. Under such a scheme, unskilled persons could be hired at a lower level but must be paid the usual level once they are employed for longer than 90-120 days. According to Hicks, this would allow for seasonal employment of teenagers and simultaneously permits companies to risk the training of those young workers who are currently viewed as lacking the labor market value.

Despite the criticism on sub-MWs for youths, Möller and König (2008, p. 16) request specific rates for younger persons and propose a differentiated MW rate between West and East Germany due to the existing productivity differences. At the same time Brenke and Eichhorst (2007, p. 130) warn of differentiation between qualifications or sectors and explain that this could risk the danger of excessive complexity associated with high levels of bureaucracy. On the other hand Siebert (2008, p. 19) emphasizes the need for differentiated MWs by age, sectors, regions and qualifications to avoid negative employment effects of a wage floor, but also states that the government would not have the information to do this in an appropriate way.

Nevertheless, it can be said, that lower MWs for young persons are appropriate despite all the criticism. The positive examples embodied by the Netherlands, as well as the negative examples associated with Sweden and Spain prove the necessity of defined rates for youths in case of a MW introduction. Furthermore, low MW rates for young workers ensure that teenagers stay in education longer which has large positive consequences for their later life and employment, as well as for society as a whole.

4.3.2 Sector specific Minimum Wages

As shown by different studies in part 4.2.1, sector specific MWs in Germany have not reduced employment in the affected industries significantly. In some regions even positive effects were found. These results are confirmed by Croucher and White (2011, p. 93) who state that systems in which MWs are set by collective bargaining are less likely to experience adverse employment impacts. According to them, one possible reason for this result could be that the outcomes of collective agreements are more likely to be linked to the current state of the labor market whereas systems with a statutory MW are more rigidly linked to economic indicators. In the debate about a statutory MW for Germany, the former chairman of the academic advisory council of the Federal Ministry of Economics, Manfred Neumann (2008, p. 17) perceives sectoral MWs as the "lesser of two evils". He explains this through the possibility that negative consequences of sectoral MWs could be observed in a decentralized fashion and thus might have moderating impacts on further wage setting processes. Axel Börsch-Supan (2008, p. 39) even considers sector specific MWs as a "political blessing", advocating for the maintenance of the present system because it shifts conflicts to a less emotional and less populist level. Furthermore, Brenke and Eichhorst (2007, p. 129) are in favor of sectoral MWs but see the major problem with the current system as the high share of low-wage workers being employed in sectors where collective wage agreements do not exist.

In conclusion it can be stated, that sectoral MWs are preferable to a nationwide uniform wage floor which can be seen in Belgium (see section 3.4) where this system is used quite successfully but also imply disadvantages for workers who are not covered by collective negotiations. For this reason a debate about a legally binding MW for the entire labor force will continually emerge as long as large numbers of workers are not covered by sector specific collective agreements, which is the current situation of the labor market in Germany.

4.3.3 Minimum Wages set by a Commission of Experts

The majority of German economists perceives the potential introduction of a legally binding MW for the whole population as very critical and recommends the retaining of the current collective bargaining system (see section 4.1.3). Nevertheless some labor market experts like Joachim Möller, director of the German Institute for Employment Research (IAB), support the idea of a statutory MW. In the case of implementation Möller demands specific minima for youths, a differentiation between the East and West German labor market but even more importantly an orientation towards the sectors in Germany which pay the lowest wages. This means that Möller recommends the introduction of a nationwide wage floor only under the condition that the level is sufficiently low (Möller and König, 2008, p. 16). Möller's view is confirmed by the former chairman of the German Council of Economic Experts, Bert Rürup (2008), who suggests a legal MW between EUR 4.07 and EUR 5.12 which meets the minimum requirements of the sociocultural existence. However, Rürup also sees the danger of an upward spiraling wage floor because of political motivations which can be observed in France (see section 3.2). According to him, it is very likely that politicians set the MW too high to ensure re-election, but neglect how harmful this would be for employment at the bottom of the labor market and especially for young workers.

For these reasons Rürup and Heilmann (2012, p. 343) support the installation of a commission of experts which should be responsible for the wage setting process. This recommendation was also stated by Möller and König (2008, p. 16) who see the chance of a depoliticization of the MW debate when installing an independent group of experts as it has been implemented in the UK (see section 3.5). Here the Low Pay Commission (LPC) advises the government and recommends the size of the MW rate. Therefore it undertakes each year consultations to gather available evidence before making proposals in its biennial review. The LPC enjoys broad support in the British population because its board consists of three labor market relations experts, three trade unionists and three employers. In contrast to Möller and König, Franz et al. (2008, p. 10) do not believe in a depolicization of the MW debate due to a commission of experts because they argue that a group like the LPC would not solve the problem but rather transfer it to the preliminary stage of selecting the board members.

Empirical evidence from the UK shows that MWs are set relatively low and thus do not lead to large disemployment effects. This is at least partly achieved with the help of an independent commission like the LPC which is why it can be stated, that a board of labor market experts is more capable of setting an appropriate MW than a national government.

5 Conclusion

As stated in the introduction, the thesis deals with the following research question:

> "What are the potential impacts of a legal minimum wage on the youth labor market in Germany and how can experiences made by other European countries help to deal with this question?"

The answer to this question was acquired through three different approaches. The first approach was to review the theory and to analyze how different models explain the way MWs affect the employment level of young persons. After considering the theoretical background, the second approach questioned whether the experiences of other European countries, which introduced or increased a statutory MW in the past, can help to estimate the potential impacts. In addition to foreign case studies, there exists empirical evidence from within Germany due to the existence of sectoral MWs. Finally, the third approach contained simulations published by various researchers who aimed to predict the potential employment effects for the total labor force. Additionally, these were supported by my own simulation designed to estimate disemployment effects particular to young workers. In the following, the most relevant results of these approaches are summarized with the aim to utilize them when answering the research question.

The analysis of the theoretical framework revealed mixed results. Some models predict negative employment effects when introducing a wage floor, while others find positive impacts or come to ambiguous conclusions. In summary, models which estimate adverse effects prevail. The relevant question for Germany would be which of the models covers best the situation on the domestic labor market. Many economists claim that the extent of monopsony power in the German labor market is rather negligible and therefore dismiss the monopsony model. According to them, the neoclassical model with its perfect competitive market is, despite its weaknesses, the most tolerable approximation to reality (Dolado et al., 1996, p. 330), which predicts disemployment effects of an implementation of a MW.

Looking on European empirical evidence revealed mixed results as well. Nevertheless, studies which find negative effects for the employment chances of young people also prevail here. Positive results were predominantly discovered in studies focusing on the British or the American labor market. The analysis showed that these countries are not comparable with the German case due to large institutional differences. On the other hand, countries that are highly similar to Germany, like France, generally face adverse effects of MWs for the employment situation of young employees. Furthermore, some studies even found negative effects on schooling. Neumark and Wascher (2010, p. 286) for example claim that a MW appears to inhibit skill acquisition by reducing educational attainment and perhaps training, which would result in lower adult wages and employment.

A further reason for the existence of positive or weak negative impacts is the concentration of short-run effects of a MW introduction. When analyzing a longer time period, many studies came to more negative labor demand elasticities. This is explained by Croucher and White (2011, p. 84) with lagged effects of a MW implementation. According to them a MW will take some time to work through the system, which is particular important in an European context as opposed to the situation in the US due to the existence of employment protection legislation which generally inhibits rapid headcount adjustment. This means that many studies underestimated the negative employment effects of a MW introduction because they only observed a short period before and after the change of the MW. Thus, in summary it can be stated that negative employment effects clearly prevail. However, due to their institutional differences, evidence from other countries cannot be directly transferred to Germany.

Nevertheless some lessons can be learned from other countries which might mitigate adverse impacts on youth employment. Subminimum wage rates for younger workers for example seem to weaken strong disemployment effects, as shown in the Netherlands. Furthermore the assignment of the responsibility to set and change the MW to an independent commission of experts seems to be beneficial, evident in the

UK where the Low Pay Commission is in charge of the MW setting process. Finally, sectoral MWs like in Belgium might also weaken potential negative effects.

This view is confirmed by empirical evidence from German studies which analyzed the employment effects of sector specific wage floors (e.g. in the construction sector). Most of these studies found low adverse effects but also showed that the group which is hit hardest by these effects is usually the group of young workers.

Analyzing the third approach to answer the research question reveals the clearest results. According to all of the papers, which estimated the potential impact of a MW introduction on the German labor market, young people would disproportionally be affected by this policy. For instance, a recent study, published by Brenke and Müller (2013), showed that 44% of the 18 to 24-year-olds receive currently less than EUR 8.50 per working hour which is the desired MW level of many political parties at the moment. Furthermore the authors of the different studies conclude that a MW would lead to large reductions in total employment ranging from 161,000 (Müller and Steiner, 2008b) to 1,189,000 (Bachmann et al., 2008). Nevertheless, none of these simulations have particularly considered the employment effects for the youth labor market. My simulation tried to close this gap. Despite the fact, that the results reached are far from being certain, the simulation revealed large negative impacts for young people as well. These depend substantially on the estimated elasticity of labor demand as well as on the relative size of the MW.

In conclusion it can be stated that the impact of a MW introduction on the youth labor market cannot be predicted with absolute certainty. Nevertheless, the theoretical framework, the European evidence and the results of the German simulations clearly point to large negative effects on youth employment.

Appendix

Table A.1: Tabular Summary of Results from French Literature

Study	Time Period(s)	Approach	Analyzed Group	Effects of MW on Youth Employment, Elasticities and further Results
Rosa (1980)[1]	1963-1979	Mincer approach (employment equations for youg persons)	15-24-years-old	negative effect: -0.61 (male youth), -0.41 (total) *criticism*: some important explanatory variables were left aside (e.g. trend variable), negative effect might be caused by other variables
Martin (1983)[1]	1963-1979	Mincer approach (employment equations for youg persons)	15-24-years-old	negative effect: -0.381 (total) *criticism*: serious problem of residuals auto-correlation
Bazen and Martin (1991)	1963-1986	modified Mincer approach (1st equation: impact of MW on average wages, 2nd equation: demand for labor)	15-24-years-old	negative but insignificant effect: -0.01 to -0.02 (total) real wage elasticity: -0.37
Skourias (1992)[1]	1968-1990	Cousineau approach	15-24-years-old	negative but insignificant effect: -0.089 to -0.148 (total)

Study	Time Period(s)	Approach	Analyzed Group	Effects of MW on Youth Employment, Elasticities and further Results
Benhayoun (1993)[1]	1968-1991	Mincer approach	15-24-years-old, focus on differences by sex	negative effect: -0.13 to -0.35 (male) not significant for female, results instable
Benhayoun (1994)[2]	1975-1990	Mincer approach	15-24-years-old	relation between MW and young persons' employment seems to exist but is very fragile (statistically not significant)
Fitoussi (1994)	1970-1989	Mincer approach	15-24-years-old	some evidence that MW have caused greater unemployment among young unskilled workers
Skourias (1995)[1]	1970-1990	different approaches (Mincer approach, Cousineau approach)	15-24-years-old	negative effect: -0.2 to -0.22 (total), results do not allow to conclude that MW contributes very significantly to youth employment decline
Dolado et al. (1996)	1981-1989	natural experiment difference-in-differences (10% increase of SMIC in 1981)	focus on low-wage regions	effect not robust and ambigous, business cycle more likely the reason for changes in youth employment

Study	Time Period(s)	Approach	Analyzed Group	Effects of MW on Youth Employment, Elasticities and further Results
Bazen and Skourias (1997)	1980-1984	natural experiment difference-in-differences (10% increase of SMIC in 1981)	young and adult workers	few robust evidence for negative effects in 1981, but negative effects on long-run (1980-1984) *criticism*: some important explanatory variables not considered (labor market policies)
Bruno and Cazes (1997)[3] and 1998)	1974-1994, 1971-1994	Mincer approach	15-24-years-old	1997 study: not significant positive employment effects 1998: not significant negative employment effects *criticism*: only some specifications differ between both studies but they lead to total different results
Abowd et al. (1997, 1999)	1981-1989	1st step: multinomial logit analysis to control for factors that might render low wage workers different from other workers, 2nd: difference-in-differences	60.000 young individuals were followed from year to year	1997: positive and negative effects, but not significant *criticism*: treatment and controll group are not significantly different, 1999: negative effects but only occasionally statistically significant

Study	Time Period(s)	Approach	Analyzed Group	Effects of MW on Youth Employment, Elasticities and further Results
Abowd et al. (2000)	1990-1998	natural experiment difference-in-differences (decrease of real labor costs due to fall of relative SMIC at beginning of 1990s)	various ages	large disemployment effects for workers newly constrained by MW relative to those with marginally higher wages, negative effect: -0.12 (men), -0.125 (women) men (25-30): -0.48 *criticism*: treatment group represents only 3-4% of the labor force
Laroque and Salanié (2000)4	1990-1999	econometrical model examining individual longitudinal data	15-24-years-old	10% increase of the MW: -290.000 jobs for young persons *criticism*: problematic assumptions, study not independent from political interests

1: Studies in French language which were analyzed by Ghellab (1998, pp. 24-28, 45-46)
2: Study cited by Croucher and White (2011, pp. 67-69)
3: Study cited by Sturn (2008, pp. 22-24)
4: Study cited by Schmid and Schulten (2006, pp. 116-117)

Source: Bazen and Martin (1991), Fitoussi (1994), Dolado et al. (1996), Bazen and Skourias (1997), Abowd et al. (1997, 1999, 2000), Bruno and Cazes (1998), Ghellab (1998), Schmid and Schulten (2006), Sturn (2008), Croucher and White (2011)

Table A.2: Tabular Summary of Results from Spanish Literature

Study	Time Period(s)	Approach	Analyzed Group	Effects of MW on Youth Employment, Elasticities and further Results
Dolado et al. (1996)	1990-1994	natural experiment sharp increase in MW for 16-year-olds (+83%), modest increase for 17-year-olds (+15%) in 1990	teens (16-19)	negative effects on teenage employment (-0.37): employers substituted away from 16- to 19-year-olds after increase of MW
Gonzalez-Guemes (1997)*	1976-1995 and 1981-1992	natural experiment (two time periods because of several methodological variations in Economically Active Population Survey)	total employment	rise in the MW has negative effect on employment particularly on employment of teenagers (16-19)
Perez-Dominguez et al. (2002)*	1981-1999	natural experiment sharp increase in MW for 16-year-olds (+83%), modest increase for 17-year-olds (+15%) in 1990	total employment in manufacturing and service industries	effect of a rise in MW on teenagers' employment is negativ and significant

Appendix

Study	Time Period(s)	Approach	Analyzed Group	Effects of MW on Youth Employment, Elasticities and further Results
Gonzalez-Guemes and Perez-Dominguez (2002)*	1963-1997	literature review compares some key trends relating MWs in Spain (e.g. Kaitz index, elasticities of different age groups)	different age groups	wage regulations, specifically those on the MW, could have negative effects on employment of individuals who commonly work on MW arrangements, notably teenagers
Blazquez et al. (2009)	2000-2008	time-series approach static and dynamic models regional adjusted Kaitz index (taking into account regional differences)	15-24-years-old	lagged effects of a MW increase, no evidence for negative effects on youth employment if regional differences and seasonal work variation is considered
Cebrian et al. (2010)*	2000-2008 and 1981-2009	time-series approach different data sets, all incorparated in the analysis through different means	total employment	no effect on employment rate, even in the case of teenagers

*: Studies in Spanish language which were analyzed in the literature review from Croucher and White (2011, pp. 70-72, 142-143)

Source: Dolado et al. (1996), Blazquez et al. (2009), Croucher and White (2011)

Table A.3: Tabular Summary of Results from Greek Literature

Study	Time Period(s)	Approach	Analyzed Group	Effects of MW on Youth Employment, Elasticities and further Results
Koutsogeorgopoulou (1994)	1962-1987	Mincer approach	total employment in manufacturing industry	negative effects of MW on total employment in manufacturing sector, but weak correlation elasticity: -0.05 to -0.11
Karageorgiu (2004)	1981-2000	time-series approach various model specifications variation between 15-19 and 20-24-year-olds relative to average adult wages	15-24-years-old	15-19: -0.09 to 0.68 (insignificant positive effects) 20-24: 0.15 to -0.25 (insignifcant negative effects) relatively more expensive young workers substituted by teenagers

Source: Koutsogeorgopoulou (1994), Karageorgiu (2004)

Table A.4: Tabular Summary of Results from Portuguese Literature

Study	Time Period(s)	Approach	Analyzed Group	Effects of MW on Youth Employment, Elasticities and further Results
Ribeiro (1993)*	1980-1990	classical equation relied on Cousineau approach	6 groups: 15-19 male&female 20-24 male&female 25-64 male&female	men (15-19): -0.082 women (15-19): -0.195 men (20-24): -0.078 women (20-24): -0.474 men (25-64): -0.018 women (25-64): -0.036 total impact of MW on youth employment: -0.1 to -0.2 (except for young women aged 20-24)
Pereira (2003)	1986-1989	natural experiment abolition of teenage sub-MW (75%) in 1987 difference-in-differences estimation	18-19 and 20-25-years-old	teen employment declined relative to employment of 30-35-year-olds elasticity: -0.2 to -0.4 substitution toward 20-25-year-olds, reduction also in the average work week for teenage employees effects stronger 1-2 years later

Study	Time Period(s)	Approach	Analyzed Group	Effects of MW on Youth Employment, Elasticities and further Results
Portugal and Cardoso (2006)	1986-1989	natural experiment abolition of teenage sub-MW (75%) in 1987 difference-in-differences estimation	15-24-years-old	major effect on teenagers of a rising MW is the reduction of separations from the employer, which more than compenstes for the reduction of accessions to new and continuing firms

*: Study in Portuguese language which was analyzed in the literature review from Ghellab (1998, pp. 31, 46)
Source: Ghellab (1998), Pereira (2003), Portugal and Cardoso (2006)

Table A.5: Tabular Summary of Results from Belgian Literature

Study	Time Period(s)	Approach	Analyzed Group	Effects of MW on Youth Employment, Elasticities and further Results
Cockx et al. (2004)	1998-2001	natural experiment differences-in-differences, focus on the effects of an income support policy	18-26-year-olds (8,630 long-term unemployed young women)	unemployment among less educated employees can be explained by a lack of demand rather than a lack of financial incentives
Marx et al. (2009)*	2004-2006	micro simulation to calculate how many are affected by fiscal and parafiscal policy, calculation of how many people work at the MW	working poor in the Flanders region	rise in the MW of even 30% would not have a significant impact on poverty reduction, since most of the working poor are working at the bottom of the MW scale and thus gain the least
Ballegeer and Duvillier (2009)*	2000-2007	international literature review from Flemish employers' organisation VOKA	all age groups without special focus on youth	MWs in Belgian are too high

Study	Time Period(s)	Approach	Analyzed Group	Effects of MW on Youth Employment, Elasticities and further Results
Van Hemel and Darquenne (2009)*	2002-2008	interviews with Belgian NEET-youngsters, qualitative sociological perspective	NEET-youngsters	other aspects (social and psychological) than financial ones (MW) act as impediments to the transition from school to work

*: Studies in Dutch and French language which were analyzed in the literature review from Croucher and White (2011), Croucher and White (2011)

Source: Cockx et al. (2004), Croucher and White (2011)

Table A.6: Tabular Summary of Results from Dutch Literature

Study	Time Period(s)	Approach	Analyzed Group	Effects of MW on Youth Employment, Elasticities and further Results
Van Soest (1994)	1984-1987	natural experiment and Meyer-Wise approach (decrease of the MW for young persons) focus on macro and micro evidence	all age groups	results of micro-econometric analysis: -0.59 (male) and -0.54 (female) in 1984, -0.51 (male) and -0.59 (female) in 1987
Koning et al. (1995)	model (no specific time period was analyzed)	equilibrium search model based on Burdett and Mortensen	all age groups	10% increase in MW increases structural unemployment from 5.2% to 10.1%.
Dolado et al. (1996)	1979-1985	natural experiment (fraction of the adult MW received by 20-year-olds and 16-year-olds was reduced significantly)	9 occupations where young workers are mostly found (17 to 22-year-olds)	cut in youth MWs did increase the relative employment of workers in those sectors most likely to be affected (agriculture and textiles), but on margin of statistical significance

Source: Van Soest (1994), Koning et al. (1995), Dolado et al. (1996)

Table A.7: Tabular Summary of Results from British Literature

Study	Time Period(s)	Approach	Analyzed Group	Effects of MW on Youth Employment, Elasticities and further Results
Bazen (1990)	1990	macroeconomic study: simulated impact that would result from an introduction of a MW	all age groups without special focus on youth	MW would cause the loss of up to 250,000 jobs
Machin and Manning (1994)	1979-1990	longitudinal data (big decline in sectoral MWs during the 1980s)	total employment in 4 low-wage sectors (catering, retail, clothing, hairdressing)	catering: positive (significant) retail: positive (insignificant) clothing: positive (insignificant) hairdressing: negative (insignificant) MW has either no or positive effects
Stewart (2002)	1998-2000	natural experiment (evaluates impact of introduction of the NMW in 1999 by using the geographical variation in wages) difference-in-differences methodology	all workers and various skill groups (two age groups: youths only (18-21) and all aged 18 and above)	after introduction of MW employment growth was not significantly lower in areas with high proportion of low-wage workers compared to areas with lower proportions, negative but insignificant effects for those aged 18-21

Study	Time Period(s)	Approach	Analyzed Group	Effects of MW on Youth Employment, Elasticities and further Results
Machin et al. (2003)	1998-1999	natural experiment difference-in-differences methodology (introduction of the NMW in April 1999) focus on residential care homes industry	low paid workers of all ages (care home sector)	MW raised wages of a large number of care home workers (reduced wage inequality), some evidence of employment reductions but insignificant effects
Stewart (2004)	1998-2003	difference-in-differences methodology focus on the effects of NMW introduction and subsequent upratings uses individual-level longitudinal data	4 demographic groups: male and female adults (22-59) and youths (18-21)	no negative effects on youth employment only negative effects for adult women (but statistically insignificant)
Dickens et al. (2010)	1999-2009	regression discontinuity focus on the impact of the transition from development rate to the adult rate	above those just a few months above and below age 22	positive and statistically significant employment effect at age 22 for low-skilled workers (hypothesis: because it is worth more to engage with the labor market)

Source: Bazen (1990), Gregg (1992), Machin and Manning (1994), Low Pay Network (1994), Ghellab (1998), Stewart (2002), Machin et al. (2003), Stewart (2004), Dickens et al. (2010), Croucher and White (2011)

Table A.8: Tabular Summary of Results from American Literature

Study	Time Period(s)	Approach	Analyzed Group	Effects of MW on Youth Employment, Elasticities and further Results
Brown et al. (1982b)	19 studies from 1970 to 1982	literature review about 19 studies assessing the MW effect on youth employment (13 time-series studies and 6 cross-section studies)	teenagers and youths	*time-series studies* (focus on teenagers): effects range from -0.296 to -0.084, even one study came to positive results (+0.256) *cross-section studies*: on average results range from -0.1 to -0.3
Meyer and Wise (1982)	1973-1987	Meyer-Wise approach (estimated what the earnings distribution would look like in the absence of MW based on the actual distribution of earnings above the legal MW)	15-24-years-old	if there had been no minimum, employment would have been higher than it was young men (16-24): +4% male teenagers (16-19): +7% black youth (16-24): +6% no evidence for earnings effect
Hall (1982)	1960-1980	focus on turnover rates among teenagers and adults (data from US	comparing adults with youths/	MW causes not long duration of unemployment for youths but high frequency of unemployment (high-

Study	Time Period(s)	Approach	Analyzed Group	Effects of MW on Youth Employment, Elasticities and further Results
		surveys comparing turnover and unemployment among teenagers and adults)	teenagers	er turnover rate which is waste of resources)
Katz and Krueger (1992)	1991	natural experiment MW increase in Texas	employees of fast-food restaurants in Texas	fast-food restaurants that had to increase pay to meet the new federal MW experienced faster employment growth (evidence for monopsony power in local labor markets in Texas)
Neumark and Wascher (1992)	1981-1991	panel-data approach	teenagers and youths in District of Columbia	teenagers (16-19): -0.1 to -0.2 youths (16-24): -0.15 to -0.2
Card and Krueger (1994)	1992	natural experiments MW increase in New Jersey, no MW increase in Pennsylvania	employees of fast-food restaurants in New Jersey and Pennsylvania	MW increase in New Jersey did not lead to employment contraction but rather positive effects on employment

Study	Time Period(s)	Approach	Analyzed Group	Effects of MW on Youth Employment, Elasticities and further Results
Currie and Fallick (1996)	1979-1987	longitudinal data focus on effects of increases in MW between 1980 and 1981 (data from National Longitudinal Survey of Youth)	15-24-years-old	increasing the MW reduced youth employment by about 3% a year afterwards (significant elasticity: -0.19 to -0.24)
Turner and Demiralp (2001)	1991-1992	multinomial logit analysis follows teens if they move out of their parents' household (federal MW increase in 1991)	15-24-years-old	MW hike significantly decreases probability of becoming idel but negative impact on school enrolment
Williams and Mills (2001)	1954-1993	same approach as Card and Krueger (1995) but using a more sophisticated dynamic specification (simple OLS and more dynamic model specifications)	teenagers	highest negative effect after 2 years: -0.45, effect disappears after 4 years, 1% rise in MW brings immediately -0.06, -0.16 after first quarter

Study	Time Period(s)	Approach	Analyzed Group	Effects of MW on Youth Employment, Elasticities and further Results
		additional using system estimation (VAR: Vector Autoregression Analysis)		
Bazen and Marimoutou (2002)	1954-1999	focusing on stochastic nature of seasonal, cyclical and trend components in teenage employment	teenagers	increases in the real MW have negative impact on teenage employment (-0.1 within the same quarter, -0.2 in long-term)
Neumark and Wascher (2003b)	1978-1998	focus on relationship between schooling and MW	15-24-years-old	positive and significant impacts of MW on proportion of workers employed but on those enrolled (it "sucks" young people out of school)

Source: Brown et al. (1982), Meyer and Wise (1982), Hall (1982), Katz and Krueger (1992), Neumark and Wascher (1992), Card and Krueger (1994), Currie and Fallick (1996), Ghellab (1998), Turner and Demiralp (2001), Williams and Mills (2001), Bazen and Marimoutou (2002), Neumark and Wascher (2003b), Croucher and White (2011)

Table A.9: Tabular Summary of Results from German Simulations

Study	Aim of the Simulation and Data Set	Effects of MW on Employment, Share of affected Workers and further Results
Kalina and Weinkopf (2006)	*MW: 7.50€* estimation: how many people would be affected after introducing a MW (what kind of sectors, what kind of companies would be affected) *data set:* SOEP (2004)	- 4.6 mio (14.6%) earn wages below 7.50€ - 7.50€: 48% of the average wage - 28.8% of all persons without vocational training would receive MW - 32.4% of 15-24-year olds would receive MW - 64.3% of low-wage workers would get MW - 45.0% of all persons with side job as main source of income would earn MW
Ragnitz and Thum (2007)	simulation of employment effects of different MWs, supposed constant elasticity: -0.75 *data set:* GLS (2001)	- employment effect (MW 6.50€): -826,000 - employment effect (MW 7.50€): -1,100,000 - 26.5% of all persons earning below 7.50€ would lose their job
Brenke and Eichhorst (2007)	estimation: how many people would be affected after introducing MW of (4.50€, 6.00€, 7.00€, 7.50€, 8.00€) *data set:* SOEP (2005)	- 3% of the labor force earn less than 4.50€, 14% less than 8.00€ - pupils and students: 15% earn less than 4.50€, 52% less than 8.00€
Müller and Steiner (2008a)	using microsimulation model STSM aim: analyzing potential MW effects on distribution of household incomes and poverty, *MW: 7.50€*	- substantial impact on wages at the bottom of the wage distribution - weak link between low hourly wages and net household income

Study	Aim of the Simulation and Data Set	Effects of MW on Employment, Share of affected Workers and further Results
	data set: SOEP (2006)	- 18-25: 22.44% affected of MW - MW ineffective in reducing poverty
Müller and Steiner (2008b)	estimated elasticities of labor demand and estimated cross price elasticities MW: 7.50€, data set: SOEP (2007)	employment effect: -161,400 (-0.59%), in case of an elasticity of goods demand of -0.5
Bachmann et al. (2008)	2 approaches combined 1st: estimation of the disemployment effects and fiscal effects for 4 different MWs data set: SOEP (2006) and BAP (2005) 2nd: telephone interviews among companies in 8 different sectors (i.a. retail, catering, haircutter) regarding expected effects of MW introduction	results 1st approach: significant disemployment effects: MW of 5.00€: -659,000; 6.00€: -832,000; 7.50€: -1,189,000; 10.00€: -1,984,000 (highest disemployment effects in security sector and haircutter sector), high costs of MW introduction in total (7.50€: -9.191 bn) 2nd results: 60% of the companies are in favor of a MW introduction; 16% would fire employees in case of a MW of 7.50€
Knabe and Schöb (2008)	standard model of a neoclassical labor market (complementarity and substitutability relationship of different types of work are not assumed) constant labor demand elasticity: -0.75 data set: SOEP (2007)	- employment effect: -842,033 (-2.60%) - students: 125,253 earn less than 5.00€ (22.3% of all students), 279,010 less than 7.50€ (49.6%) - substantial share of low-wage employment consists of students and pensioners that try to earn some money "at the side"

Study	Aim of the Simulation and Data Set	Effects of MW on Employment, Share of affected Workers and further Results
Bauer et al. (2009)	simulation of the potential employment and fiscal effects, based on estimated labor demand elasticities obtained from a structural labor demand model *data set*: SOEP (2007) and BAP (2006)	- employment effect: -860,000 (-3.34%) - employment losses are concentrated among low- and semi-skilled full-time workers - MW will result in a significant fiscal burden
Müller (2009b)	simulation based on estimated labor demand elasticities for different typs of jobs and different qualification levels *data set*: SOEP (2006) and VSE (2006)	- MW: 7.50 - employment effect: -290,600 (-1.43%) - for low-wage workers: -111,400 - for employees working part-time: -40,300
Brautzsch and Schultz (2013)	estimation: how many people would be affected after introducing a MW of 8.50€ (what kind of sectors, what kind of job types), *data set*: SOEP (2011)	- total: 14.1% get less than 8.50€ (by contract) - total: 19.2% earn less than 8.50€ (effectively) - low-wage workers: 59% receive less than 8.50€
Brenke and Müller (2013)	estimation: how many people would be affected after introducing a MW of 8.50€ and 10.00€ (depending on sector, job type, qualification, age and sex) *data set*: SOEP (2011)	- youths (18-24): 44% earn less than 8.50€, 62% earn less than 10.00€ - total: 17% earn less than 8.50?, 26% earn less than 10.00€

BAP: Beschäftigtenpanel of the German Institute for Employment Research (IAB)
GLS: Gehalts- und Lohnstrukturerhebung of the German Federal Statistical Office
SOEP: German Socio-Economic Panel of the German Institute for Economic Research (DIW)
VSE: Verdienst- und Strukturerhebung of the German Federal Statistical Office

Table A.10: Tabular Summary of Results from German Studies concerning Sectoral MWs

Study	Analyzed Sector and used Approach	Effects of MW on Employment, Share of affected Workers and further Results
König and Möller (2007)	*sector: main construction industry* *natural experiment*: sector specific MW introduction in 1997 (17.00 DM in West, 15.64 DM in East Germany) *control group*: employees earning slightly above the MW, difference-in-differences *data set*: microdata from the employment statistics of the IAB (panel data) *analyzed time period*: 1994-1997	*results for East Germany*: negative employment effects, substantial changes in the wage structure (significant wage increases) *results for West Germany*: positive but weak significant employment effects, spillover effects (rise of wages of control group) *explanation*: relative MW in East higher than in West GER, displacement of foreign workers in West GER (lost wage cost advantage)
Bachmann and Kluve (2008)	*sector: letter services* *interviews*: with the aim to study the short-term and the expected long-term consequences of sector specific MW introduction in 2008 (West: 9.80€, East: 9€), survey 1 month after implementation	*short-term results*: 1.8% reported positive effects, 69.7% negative effects *expected long-term effects*: 11% expect positive effects, 65.1% negative effects *reactions concerning MW introduction*: *short-term*: 13% price increase, 30% job cuts, 3.5% hiring of workers

Study	Analyzed Sector and used Approach	Effects of MW on Employment, Share of affected Workers and further Results
	data set: survey among 113 companies, managers were interviewed, conducted by Forsa Institute *time period of survey*: February 2008	*expected long-term*: 36.3% price increase, 52.8% job cuts, 12% hiring of workers *conclusion*: significant negative employment effects (expected), since price increase almost not possible
Aretz et al. (2012)	*sector*: roofing industry *natural experiment*: sector specific MW introduction in 1997, 2003 nationwide same MW, 2011: 11.00€ *2 control groups*: 1. employees of a similar sector (installation business) and 2. employees earning slightly above the MW, difference-in-differences *different data sets*: i.a. microdata from the employment statistics of the IAB (panel data), surveys by telephone *analyzed time period*: 1994-1996 (before introduction), 1997-2007 (afterwards)	*employment effect East GER (for workers affected by MW)*: -0.7% (in comparison to 1st control group), -2.8% (2nd control group) *employment effect West*: +1.5% (1st control group), -6% (2nd control group), 30% reported higher motivation due to MW *explanation for employment effects in West*: assumptions were violated *further results*: some companies did not pay MW (more controls needed) *conclusion*: on total no negative employment effects, but decreasing probability of continuing employment for workers earning the MW, workers earning above MW profit from it. MW could increase shortage of skilled workers due to lack of wage differentiation

Study	Analyzed Sector and used Approach	Effects of MW on Employment, Share of affected Workers and further Results
Müller (2012)	*sector*: main construction industry *literature review*: studies concerning different sectors in construction industry which were conducted on behalf of German Federal Ministry of Labor and Social Affairs *common features of the studies*: all use natural experiment (sectoral MW introduction in 1997) in conjunction with difference-in-differences	*general results*: MW has no significant impact on employment in this industry (weak negative employment effects in East GER), for adult workers in West even positive effects, but large negative consequences for youths (18-25, especially in East) *problem of most of the studies*: data base, general development of employment in this industry (declining trend since mid 1990s), many results therefore biased

List of References

Abowd, J., Kramarz, F., Lemieux, T., Margolis, D. (1997), Minimum Wages and Youth Employment in France and the United States, in: NBER Working Paper, No. 6111.

Abowd, J., Kramarz, F., Margolis, D. (1999), Minimum Wages and Youth Employment in France and the United States, in: NBER Working Paper, No. 6996.

Abowd, J., Kramarz, F., Margolis, D., Philippon, T. (2000), The Tail of Two Countries – Minimum Wages and Employment in France and the United States, IZA Discussion Paper, No. 203.

Acemoglu, D., Pischke, J. (1999), The Structure of Wages and Investment in General Training, in: Journal of Political Economy, No. 107, pp. 539-572.

Ackerman, C., Klaassen, I. (1998), The Lower End of the Labor Market 1998, The Hague: Ministry of Social Affairs and Employment.

Aretz, B., Arntz, M., Gregory, T., Rammer, C. (2012), Der Mindestlohn im Dachdeckerhandwerk – Auswirkungen auf Beschäftigung, Arbeitnehmerschutz und Wettbewerb, in: ZEW Discussion Paper, No.12-060.

Ashenfelter, O., Farber, H., Ransom, M. (2010), Modern Models of Monopsony in Labor Markets – A Brief Survey, in: IZA Discussion Paper Series, No. 4915.

Bachmann, R., Bauer, T., Kluve, J., Schaffner, S., Schmidt, C. (2008), Mindestlöhne in Deutschland – Beschäftigungswirkungen und fiskalische Effekte, in: RWI Materialien, No. 43.

Bachmann, R., Kluve, J. (2008), Auswirkungen der Einführung des Postmindestlohns – Befragung von Unternehmen der Branche Briefdienstleistungen, in: RWI Projektberichte, Forschungsvorhaben des Bundesministeriums für Wirtschaft und Technologie, Endbericht.

Ballegeer, D., Duvillier, G. (2009), Minimumloon bron van Werkloosheid, in: VOKA position paper, Press release 01.03.2009, http://statbel.fgov.be/nl/binaries/ac1237_nl\%5B1\%5D_tcm325-45932.pdf [retrieved on 15.08.2013].

Bauer, T., Schmidt, C. (2007), Mindestlöhne und das Entsendegesetz, in: RWI Positionen, Vol. 87, No. 2.

Bauer, T., Kluve, J., Schaffner, S., Schmidt, C. (2009), Fiscal Effects of Minimum Wages – An Analysis for Germany, in: German Economic Review, Vol. 10, pp. 224-242.

Bazen, S. (1990), On the Employment Effects of Introducing a National Minimum Wage, in: British Journal of Industrial Relations, Vol. 28, No. 2, pp. 215-226.

Bazen, S., Marimoutou, V. (2002), Looking for a Needle in a Haystick? A Re-Examination of the Time Series Relationship between Teenage Employment and Minimum Wages in the United States, in: Oxford Bulletin of Economics & Statistics, Vol. 64, Supplement 1, pp. 699-725.

Bazen, S., Martin, J. (1991), The Impact of the Minimum Wage on Earnings and Employment in France, in: OECD Economic Studies, Vol. 16, pp. 199-221.

Bazen, S., Skourias, N. (1997), Is there a negative Effect of Minimum Wages on Youth Employment in France?, in: European Economic Review, Vol. 41, pp. 723-732.

BDA (ed.) (2013), Balance in der Tarifautonomie wahren – Position der Arbeitgeber zur Mindestlohndebatte, Bundesvereinigung der Deutschen Arbeitgeber, Präsidiumsbeschluss zum Mindestlohn, Press release 20.04.2007, http://www.arbeitgeber.de/www/arbeitgeber.nsf/res/BDA_Praesidiumsbeschluss.pdf/\$file/BDA_Praesidiumsbeschluss.pdf [retrieved on 24.09.2013].

Bell, D., Blanchflower, D. (2010), Youth Unemployment – Déjà Vu?, in: IZA Discussion Paper, No. 4705.

Benhayoun, G. (1993), Salaire minimum et emploi des jeunes en France: une relation confirmée mais fragile, in: Actes du Colloque International: Analyse Économique des bas Salaires et des Effets du Salaire Minimum, pp. 107-126.

Benhayoun, G. (1994), The Impact of Minimum Wages on Youth Employment in France Revisited – A Note on the Robustness of the Relationship, in: International Journal of Manpower, Vol. 15, No. 2, Iss. 3, pp. 82-85.

Bertola, G., Driffill, J., James, H., Sinn, H.-W., Sturm, J.-E., Valentinyi, A. (2013), Labour Market Reforms and Youth Unemployment, in: EEAG (ed.): The EEAG Report on the European Economy, Munich: CESifo, pp. 73-94.

Bhaskar, V., Manning, A., To, T. (2002), Oligopsony and Monopsonistic Competition in Labor Markets, in: Journal of Economic Perspectives, Vol. 16, No. 2, pp. 155-174.

Bhaskar, V., To, T. (1999), Minimum Wages for Ronald McDonald Monopsonies – A Theory of Monopsonistic Competition, in: The Economic Journal, Vol. 109, Iss. 455, pp. 190-203.

Blanchflower, D., Freeman, B. (2000), The Declining Economic Status of Young Workers in OECD Countries, in: NBER (ed.): Youth Employment and Joblessness in Advanced Countries, Chicago: University of Chicago Press, pp. 19-56.

Blázquez, M., Llorente, R., Moral, J. (2009), Minimum Wage and Youth Employment Rates in Spain – New Evidence for the Period 2000-2008, in: Economic Analysis Working Paper Series, No. 2, pp. 1-35.

Börsch-Supan, A. (2008), Mindestlöhne vermeiden Armut nicht, in: ifo Schnelldienst, Special Issue, Vol. 61, No. 6, München: ifo Institut für Wirtschaftsforschung, pp. 37-40.

Brautzsch, H., Schultz, B. (2013), Mindestlohn von 8,50 Euro – Wie viele verdienen weniger, und in welchen Branchen arbeiten sie?, in: IWH-Pressemitteilung, No. 19.

Brenke, K., Eichhorst, W. (2007), Mindestlohn für Deutschland nicht sinnvoll, in: DIW Wochenbericht, Vol. 74, Iss. 9, pp. 121-131.

Brenke, K., Müller, K. (2013), Gesetzlicher Mindestlohn – Kein verteilungspolitisches Allheilmittel, in: DIW Wochenbericht, No. 39/2013.

Brown, C., Gilroy, C., Kohen, A. (1982a), The Effect of the Minimum Wage on Employment and Unemployment – A Survey, in: NBER Working Paper Series, No. 1982.

Brown, C., Gilroy, C., Kohen, A. (1982b), Time-Series Evidence of the Effect of the Minimum Wage on Youth Employment and Unemployment, in: The Journal of Human Resources, Vol. 18, No. 1, pp. 3-46.

Bruno, C., Cazes, S. (1997), Le Chômage des Jeunes en France – Un État des Lieux, in: Revue de L'OFCE, No. 62.

Bruno, C., Cazes, S. (1998), French Youth Unemployment – An Overview, in: ILO Employment and Training Papers, Vol. 23.

Bundesrat (ed.) (2013), Entwurf eines Gesetzes über die Festsetzung des Mindestlohns – Mindestlohngesetz – MinLohnG, in: Bundesrat Drucksache 136/13.

Bundesregierung (ed.) (2013), Mindestlöhne für Steinmetze und Bildhauer, Press release 18.09.2013, http://www.bundesregie rung. de/Content/DE/Artikel/2013/09/2013-09-18-mindestlohn-steinmetze.html [retrieved on 20.09.2013].

Bündnis 90/Die Grünen (ed.) (2013), Zeit für einen grünen Wandel – Teilhaben – Einmischen – Zukunft schaffen, Bundestagswahlprogramm 2013, Berlin, Press release 13.06.2013, http://www.gruene.de/fileadmin/user_upload/Dokumente/ Wahlprogramm/Wahlprogramm-barrierefrei.pdf [retrieved on 20.08.2013].

Burgess, P. (2006), Der gesetzliche Mindestlohn in Großbritannien, in: Schulten, T. (ed.): Mindestlöhne in Europa, Hamburg: VSA-Verlag, pp. 31-55.

List of References

Cahuc, P., Zylberberg, A. (2004), Labor Economics, Massachusetts: MIT Press.

Card, D., Krueger, A., (1994), Minimum Wages and Employment – A Case Study of the Fast-Food Industry in New Jersey and Pennsylvania, in: The American Economic Review, Vol. 84, No. 4, pp. 772-793.

Card D., Krueger, A. (1997), Myth and Measurement – The New Economics of the Minimum Wage, Princeton: Princeton University Press.

CDU/CSU (ed.) (2013): Gemeinsam erfolgreich für Deutschland – Regierungsprogramm 2013-2017, Press release 18.06.2013, http://www.cdu.de/sites/default/files/media/dokumente/cdu_regierungsprogramm_2013-2017.pdf [retrieved on 20.08.2013].

Cebrian, I., Pitarch, J., Rodriguez, C., Toharia, L. (2010), Análisis de los Efectos del Aumento del Salario Minimo Sobre el Empleo de la Economica Espanola, in: Revista de Economia Laboral, Vol. 7, pp. 1-37.

Cockx, B., Robin, S., Goebel, C. (2006), Income Support Policies for Part-Time Workers – A Stepping-Stone to Regular Jobs? An Application to Young Long-Term Unemployed Women in Belgium, in: IZA Discussion Paper, No. 2432.

Cousineau, J., Tessier, D., Vaillancourt, F. (1992), The Impact of the Ontarian Minimum Wage on the Unemployment of Women and the Young in Ontario – A Note, in: The Journal of Industrial Relations, Vol. 47, No. 3, pp. 559-566.

Croucher, R., White, G. (2011), The Impact of Minimum Wages on the Youth Labour Market – An International Literature Review for the Low Pay Commission, in: Project Report, London: The Low Pay Commission.

Currie, J., Fallick, B. (1996), The Minimum Wage and the Employment of Youth – Evidence from NLSY, in: The Journal of Human Resources, Vol. 31, No. 2, pp. 404-428.

Danziger, L. (2007), The Elasticity of Labor Demand and the Minimum Wage, in: IZA Discussion Paper, No. 3150.

DGB (ed.) (2013), Niedriglohn macht Deutschland arm – Arm trotz Arbeit - Deutschland braucht den Mindestlohn, http://www.mindestlohn.de/ [retrieved on 23.09.2013].

Dickens, R., Riley, R., Wilkinson, D. (2010), The Impact on Employment of the Age Related Increases in the National Minimum Wage, in: Report prepared for the Low Pay Commission, London: Low Pay Commission.

Die Linke (ed.) (2013): 100% sozial – Wahlprogramm zur Bundestagswahl 2013, Dresden, Press release 16.06.2013, http://www.die-linke.de/fileadmin/download/wahlen2013/bundestagswahlprogramm/bundestagswahl-programm2013_langfassung.pdf [retrieved on 20.08.2013].

Dietrich, H. (2012), Youth Unemployment in Europe – Theoretical Considerations and Empirical Findings, Berlin: Verlag der Friedrich-Ebert-Stiftung.

Dolado, J., Kramarz, F., Machin, S., Manning, A., Margolis, D., Teulings, C. (1996), The Economic Impact of Minimum Wages in Europe, in: Economic Policy Vol. 11, No. 23, pp. 317-372.

Dressel, C. (2005), Datenreport zur Gleichstellung von Frauen und Männern in der Bundesrepublik Deutschland, im Auftrag von: Bundesministerium für Familie, Senioren, Frauen und Jugend, München: Init.

Eichhorst, W. (2006), Kombilöhne und Mindestlöhne als Instrumente der Beschäftigungspolitik – Erfahrungen und Handlungsoptionen, in: IZA Discussion Paper, No. 2120.

Eichhorst, W., Hinte, H., Rinne, U. (2013), Jugendarbeitslosigkeit in Europa – Status Quo und (keine?) Perspektiven, in: IZA Standpunkte, No. 57.

Eurofund (ed.) (2012), NEETs – Young People not in Employment, Education or Training – Characteristics, Costs and Policy Responses in Europe, Luxembourg: Publications Office of the European Union.

Eurostat (ed.) (2013a), Unemployment Rate by Sex and Age Groups, Press release 30.08.2013, http://appsso.eurostat.ec.europa. eu/nui/show.do?dataset=une_rt_m\&lang=en [retrieved on 10.09.2013].

Eurostat (ed.) (2013b), Young people not in employment and not in any education and training, Press release: 30.08.2013, http://appsso. eurostat.ec.europa.eu/nui/show.do [retrieved on 10.09.2013].

Eurostat (ed.) (2013c), Employment (Main Characteristics and Rates) – Annual Averages, Press release 10.07.2013, http:// appsso.eurostat.ec.europa.eu/nui/show.do?dataset=lfsi_ emp_a\&lang=en [retrieved on 10.09.2013].

FDP (ed.) (2013): Bürgerprogramm 2013 – Damit Deutschland stark bleibt, Nürnberg, Press release 01.05.2013, http://www.fdp. de/files/408/B_rgerprogramm_A5_Online_2013-07-23.pdf [retrieved on 20.08.2013].

Fitoussi, J. (1994), Wage Distribution and Unemployment – The French Experience, in: American Economic Review, Vol. 84, No. 2, pp. 59-64.

Fitzenberger, B. (2009), Anmerkungen zur Mindestlohndebatte – Elastizitäten, Strukturparameter und Topfschlagen, in: Zeitschrift für ArbeitsmarktForschung, Vol. 42, Iss. 1, May, pp. 85-92.

Fotoniata, E., Moutos, T. (2010), Greece – Neglect and Resurgence of Minimum Wage Policy, in: Vaughan-Whitehead, D. (ed.): The Minimum Wage revisited in the enlarged EU, Geneva: International Labour Organization, pp. 213-243.

Franz, W., Weder di Mauro, B., Wiegard, W. (2008), Hände weg vom Mindestlohn, in: ifo Schnelldienst, Special Issue, Vol. 61, No. 6, München: ifo Institut für Wirtschaftsforschung, pp. 8-12.

Frayne, C., Goodman, A. (2004), The Impact of Introducing a National Minimum Wage for 16 and 17 Year Olds on Employment and Education Outcomes, in: A Report for the Low Pay Commission, London: LPC publishing.

Freeman, R., Wise, D. (1982), The Youth Labor Market Problem – Its Nature, Causes, and Consequences, in: Freeman, R., Wise, D. (eds.): The Youth Labor Market Problem – Its Nature Causes and Consequences, NBER Books, Chicago: University of Chicago Press, pp. 1-16.

Fuest, C. (2008), Mindestlohn – Bloß nicht, in: ifo Schnelldienst, Special Issue, Vol. 61, No. 6, München: ifo Institut für Wirtschaftsforschung, pp. 25-27.

Gautié, J. (2010), France – Towards the End of an Active Minimum Wage Policy?, in: Vaughan-Whitehead, D. (ed.): The Minimum Wage revisited in the enlarged EU, Geneva: International Labour Organization, pp. 153-182.

German Federal Bureau of Statistics (ed.) (2009), Niedrigeinkommen und Erwerbstätigkeit, Wiesbaden: Statistisches Bundesamt.

German Federal Bureau of Statistics (ed.) (2013), Mindestlöhne in Deutschland,

Press release 01.05.2013, https://www.destatis.de/DE/ZahlenFakten/GesamtwirtschaftUmwelt/VerdiensteArbeitskosten/Mindestloehne/Tabellen/MindestlohnDeutschland.html [retrieved on 20.09.2013].

Ghellab, Y. (1998), Minimum Wages and Youth Unemployment, in: Employment and Training Papers, Geneva: International Labour Office, No. 26.

Gonzalez-Guemes, I. (1997), Los Efectos del Salario Minimo Sobre el Empleo de Adolescentes, in: Cuadernos Economicos de I.C.E., Vol. 63, pp. 31-48.

Gonzalez-Guemes, I., Perez-Dominguez, C. (2002), El Efecto de las Regulaciones Salariales Sobre el Empleo – El Caso de Los Salarios Minimos, in: Boletin Economico de I.C.E., No. 2640, pp. 37-43.

Güth, W., Kliemt, H. (2008), (Mindest)Standards als Koordinationshilfe – Zur Debatte um Mindestlöhne, in: ifo Schnelldienst, Special Issue, Vol. 61, No. 6, München: ifo Institut für Wirtschaftsforschung, pp. 49-52.

Hall, R. (1982), The Minimum Wage and Job Turnover in Markets for Young Workers, in: Freeman, R., Wise, D. (eds.): The Youth Labor Market Problem – Its Nature, Causes, and Consequences, Chicago: University of Chicago Press, pp. 475-498.

Hamermesh, D. (1995), Myth and Measurement – The New Economics of the Minimum Wage – Comment, in: Industrial and Labor Relations Review, Vol. 48, No. 4, pp. 835-838.

Harris, J., Todardo, M. (1970), Migration, Unemployment and Development – A Two-Sector Analysis, in: The American Economic Review, Vol. 60, No. 1, pp. 126-142.

Hashimoto, M. (1982), Minimum Wage Effects on Training on the Job, in: American Economic Review, Vol. 72, Iss. 5, pp. 1070-1087.

Heckman, J., Borjas, G. (1980), Does Unemployment cause Future Unemployment? Definitions, Questions and Answers from a Continuous Time Model of Heterogeneity and State Dependence; in: Economica, Vol. 47, No. 2, pp. 247-283.

Helmstädter, E. (2008), Zur Mikroökonomik des Arbeitsangebots, in: ifo Schnelldienst, Special Issue, Vol. 61, No. 6, pp. 52-56, München: ifo Institut für Wirtschaftsforschung.

Hicks, M. (2010), Who Lost Jobs when the Minimum Wage Rose?, in: CBER Business Brief, Ball State University, February.

ILS (ed.) (2013), Der Verband Instore und Logistik Services e.V. (ILS) – Hintergründe und Fakten, Press release 08.07.2013, http://ils-verband.de/uploads/media/ILS_-_Hintergruende_und_Fakten_2013-07-08.pdf [retrieved on 24.09.2013].

Infratest dimap (ed.) (2013), Einführung eines gesetzlichen Mindestlohns – Eine Studie von infratest dimap im Auftrag des DGB, Press release 12.06.2013, Fehler!Hyperlink-Referenzungültig. [retrieved on 24.09. 2013]

Initiative Mindestlohn (ed.) (2013), Initiative Mindestlohn – Kein Lohn unter 8.50 €, Start of the campaign January 2006, https://www.initiative-mindestlohn.de [retrieved on 23.09.2013].

Kaitz, H. (1970), Experience of the Past – The National Minimum Wage, in: U.S. Department of Labor, Bureau of Labor Statistics (ed.): Youth Unemployment and Minimum Wages, No. 1657, pp. 30-54.

Kalina, T., Weinkopf, C. (2006), Einführung eines gesetzlichen Mindestlohns in Deutschland – eine Modellrechnung für das Jahr 2004, in: Institut Arbeit und Technik Jahrbuch 2006, pp. 97-109.

Kalina, T., Weinkopf, C. (2012), Niedriglohnbeschäftigung 2010 – Fast jede/r Vierte arbeitet für Niedriglohn, in: IAQ-Report, No. 2012-01.

Karageorgiou, L. (2004), The Impact of Minimum Wages on Youth and Teenage Employment in Greece, in: Spoudai, Vol. 54, pp. 39-67.

Katz, F., Krueger, A. (1992), The Effect of the Minimum Wage on the Fast-Food Industry, in: Industrial and Labor Relations Review, Vol. 46, No. 1, pp. 6-21.

Kennan, J. (1995), The Elusive Effects of Minimum Wages, in: Journal of Economic Literature, Vol. 33, pp. 1949-1965.

Kluve, J., Schmidt, C. (2007), Mindestlöhne ohne Reue – Eine aussichtsreiche Option für Deutschland?, in: RWI Positionen, No. 22.

Knabe, A., Schöb, R. (2008), Minimum Wage Incidence – The Case of Germany, in: CESifo Working Paper, No. 2432.

König, M., Möller, J. (2007), Mindestlohneffekte des Entsendegesetzes – Eine Mikrodatenanalyse für die deutsche Bauwirtschaft, in: IAB Discussion Paper, No. 30/2007.

Koning, P., Ridder, G., Van den Berg, G. (1995), Structural and Frictional Unemployment in an Equilibrium Search Model with Heterogeneous Agents, in: Journal of Applied Econometrics, Vol. 10, pp. 133-151.

Korenman, S., Neumark, D. (1997), Cohort Crowding and Youth Labor Markets – A Cross-National Analysis, in: NBER Working Paper Series, No. 6031.

Koutsogeorgopoulou, V. (1994), The Impact of Minimum Wages on Industrial Wages and Employment in Greece, in: International Journal of Manpower, Vol. 15, No. 2, pp. 86-99.

Laroque, G., Salanié, B. (2000), Une Décomposition du Non-Emploi en France, in: Économie et Statistique, No. 331, pp. 47-66.

Lechthaler, W., Snower, D. (2008), Mindestlöhne und Humankapital, in: ifo Schnelldienst, Special Issue, Vol. 61, No. 6, München: ifo Institut für Wirtschaftsforschung, pp. 43-44.

Lovell, M. (1972), The Minimum Wage, Teenage Unemployment, and the Business Cycle, in: Western Economic Journal, Vol. 10, No. 4, pp. 414-427.

Low Pay Commission (ed.) (2005), National Minimum Wage, in: Low Pay Commission Report 2005.

Low Pay Commission (ed.) (2010), National Minimum Wage, in: Low Pay Commission Report 2010.

Machin, S., Manning, A. (1994), The Effects of Minimum Wages on Wage Dispersions and Employment – Evidence from the U.K. Wages Councils, in: Industrial and Labor Relations Review, Vol. 47, No. 2, pp. 319-329.

Machin S., Manning, A., Rahman, L. (2003), Where the Minimum Wage Bites Hard – Introduction of Minimum Wages to a Low Wage Sector, in: Journal of the European Economic Association, Vol. 1, No. 1, pp. 152-180.

Manzoni, A., Mooi-Reci, I. (2011), Early Unemployment and Subsequent Career Complexity – A Sequence-Based Perspective, in: Wagner, G., Wagner, J. (eds.), Schmollers Jahrbuch – Journal of Applied Social Science Studies, Vol. 131, Iss. 2, Berlin: Duncker & Humblot, pp. 339-348.

Martin, G. (2009), A Portrait of the Youth Labor Market in 13 Countries – 1980-2007, in: Monthly Labor Review, United States Department of Labor, Bureau of Labor Statistics, Vol. 132, pp. 3-21.

Martin, J. (1983), Effects of the Minimum Wage on the Youth Labor Market in North America and France, in: OECD Occasional Studies, pp. 45-65.

Marx, I., Verbist, G., Vandenbroucke, P., Bogaerts, K., Vanhille, J. (2009), De Werkende Armen in Vlaanderen – Een Vergeten Groep?, in: CSB-Endreport, Centrum voor Sociaal Beleid Herman Deleeck Universiteit Antwerpen.

Metcalf, D. (2007), Why has the British Minimum Wage had little or no Impact on Employment, in: Centre for Economic Performance Discussion Paper, No. 78.

Meyer, R., Wise, D. (1982), The Effects of the Minimum Wage on the Employment and Earnings of Youth, in: NBER Working Paper Series, No. 849.

Mincer, J. (1976), Unemployment Effects of Minimum Wages, in: Journal of Political Economy, Vol. 84, No. 4, pp. 87-104.

Möller, J. (2012), Minimum Wages in German Industries – What does the Evidence tell us so far?, in: Journal for Labour Market Research, Vol. 45, Iss. 3-4, pp. 187-199.

Möller, J., König, M. (2008), Ein Plädoyer für Mindestlöhne mit Augenmaß, in: ifo Schnelldienst, Special Issue, Vol. 61, No. 6, München: ifo Institut für Wirtschaftsforschung, pp. 13-16.

Möschel, W. (2008), Mindestlöhne – Irrweg aus juristischer Perspektive, in: ifo Schnelldienst, Special Issue, Vol. 61, No. 6, München: ifo Institut für Wirtschaftsforschung, pp. 28-30.

Moser, C., Stähler, N. (2009), Spillover Effects of Minimum Wages in a Two-Sector Search Model, in: Deutsche Bundesbank Discussion Paper Series – Economic Studies, No. 1.

Mroz, T., Savage, T. (2006), The Long-Term Effects of Youth Unemployment, in: The Journal of Human Resources, Vol. 41, No. 2, pp. 259-293.

Mueller, D. (2008), Lohndumping und Mindestlöhne, in: Mindestlöhne – Für und Wider, in: ifo Schnelldienst, Special Issue, Vol. 61, No. 6, München: ifo Institut für Wirtschaftsforschung, pp. 23-25.

Müller, K. (2009a), How Robust are Simulated Employment Effects of a Legal Minimum Wage in Germany? A Comparison of different Data Sources and Assumptions, in: DIW Discussion Papers, No. 900.

Müller, K. (2009b), Wie groß sind die Beschäftigungsverluste aufgrund eines allgemeinen Mindestlohns?, in: DIW Wochenbericht, No. 26, pp. 430-433.

Müller, K. (2012), Mindestlohn im Bauhauptgewerbe – Beschäftigungseffekte nicht nachweisbar, in: DIW-Wochenbericht, Vol. 79, Iss. 47, pp. 16-21.

Müller, K., Steiner, V. (2008a), Would a Legal Minimum Wage Reduce Poverty? – A Microsimulation Study for Germany, in: DIW Discussion Papers, Vol. 791.

Müller, K., Steiner, V. (2008b), Mindestlöhne kosten Arbeitsplätze – Jobverluste vor allem bei Geringverdienern, in: DIW Wochenbericht, No. 30, July, pp. 418-423.

Neumann, M. (2008), Flächendeckender Mindestlohn – Ordnungspolitischer Sündenfall par excellence, in: ifo Schnelldienst, Special Issue, Vol. 61, No. 6, München: ifo Institut für Wirtschaftsforschung, pp. 16-18.

Neumark, D., Nizalova, O. (2004), Minimum Wage Effects in the Longer Run, in: IZA Discussion Paper, No. 1428.

Neumark, D., Wascher, W. (1992), Employment Effects of Minimum and Sub-Minimum Wages – Panel Data on State Minimum Wage Laws, in: Industrial and Labor Relations Review, Vol. 46, No. 1, pp. 55-81.

Neumark, D., Wascher, W. (1993), Employment Effects of Minimum and Subminimum Wages – Reply to Card, Katz and Krueger, in: NBER Working Paper, No. 4570.

Neumark, D., Wascher, W. (2003a), Minimum Wages, Labor Market Institutions, and Youth Employment – A Cross-National Analysis, in: Industrial and Labor Relations Review, Vol. 57, No. 2, pp. 223-248.

Neumark, D., Wascher, W. (2003b), Minimum Wages and Skill Acquisition – Another Look at Schooling Effects, in: Economics of Education Review, Vol. 22, No. 1, pp. 1-10.

Neumark, D., Wascher, W. (2006), Minimum Wages and Employment – A Review of Evidence from the New Minimum Wage Research, in: NBER Working Paper Series, No. 12663.

Neumark, D., Wascher, W. (2010), Minimum Wages, Massachusetts: MIT Press.

OECD (ed.) (1994), The OECD Jobs Study – Facts, Analysis, Strategies, Paris: OECD Publishing.

OECD (ed.) (1998), OECD Employment Outlook 1998, Paris: OECD Publishing.

OECD (ed.) (2010), Education at a Glance 2010 – OECD Indicators, Paris: OECD Publishing.

OECD (ed.) (2012), OECD Employment Outlook 2012, Paris: OECD Publishing.

OECD (ed.) (2013a), Real Minimum Wages, OECD.StatExtracts, Data extracted on 11.09.2013, `http://stats.oecd.org/Index.aspx?DataSetCode=RMW` [retrieved on 12.09. 2013]

OECD (ed.) (2013b), Minimum relative to Average Wages of Full-Time Workers, OECD.StatExtracts, Data extracted on 11.09.2013, `http://stats.oecd.org/Index.aspx?DataSetCode=MIN2AVE` [retrieved on 12.09.2013]

O'Higgins, N. (1997), The Challenge of Youth Unemployment, in: Employment & Training Papers, No. 7.

Pereira, S. (2003), The Impact of Minimum Wage Effects on Youth Unemployment in Portugal, in: European Economic Review, Vol. 47, pp. 229-244.

Perez-Dominguez, C., Gonzalez-Guemes, I., De Prada Moraga, M. (2002), Los Efectos Simultáneos del Salario Minimo Sobre el Empleo – La Participación y la Tasa de Paro de los Adolescentes Espanoles, in: Moneda y Credito, No. 215, pp. 225-246.

Portugal, P., Cardoso, A. (2006), Disentangling the Minimum Wage Puzzle – An Analysis of Worker Accessions and Separations, in: Journal of the European Economic Association, Vol. 4, No. 5, pp. 988-1013

Rabin, M. (1993), Incorporating Fairness into Game Theory and Economics, in: American Economic Review, Vol. 83, No. 5, pp. 1281-1302.

Raddatz, G., Wolf, S. (2007), Irrglaube Mindestlöhne – Trügerische Hoffnung, zerstörte Beschäftigungschancen, in: Stiftung Marktwirtschaft – Argumente zu Marktwirtschaft und Politik, No. 99.

Ragnitz, J, Thum, M. (2007), The Empirical Relevance of Minimum Wages for the Low-Wage Sector in Germany, in: CESifo Forum, Vol. 8, Iss. 2, pp. 35-37.

Ragnitz, J, Thum, M. (2008), Beschäftigungswirkungen von Mindestlöhnen – Eine Erläuterung zu den Berechnungen des ifo Instituts, in: ifo Schnelldienst, Vol. 61, No. 1, pp. 16-20.

Recio, A. (2006), Der gesetzliche Mindestlohn in Spanien, in: Schulten, T. (ed.): Mindestlöhne in Europa, Hamburg: VSA-Verlag, pp. 127-147.

Ribeiro, M. (1993), Le Salaire Minimum au Portugal – Les Incidences sur L'Emploi, in: Actes du Colloque International (ed.): Analyse Économique des Bas Salaires et des Effets du Salaire Minimum, October, pp. 876-896.

Robinson, J. (1969), The Economics of Imperfect Competition, 2nd edition, London: Macmillan.

Rosa, J. (1980), Les Effets du SMIC sur L'Emploi et la Participation des Jeunes, in: Vie et Sciences Économiques, pp. 17-28.

Rürup, B. (2008), Für einen moderaten allgemeinen Mindestlohn, in: ifo Schnelldienst, Special Issue, Vol. 61, No. 6, München: ifo Institut für Wirtschaftsforschung, pp. 5-7.

Rürup, B., Heilmann, D. (2012), Arbeitsmarktreformen – Was noch zu tun bleibt, in: Wirtschaftsdienst, Vol. 92, Iss. 5, pp. 339-344.

Rycx, F., Kampelmann, S. (2012), Who earns Minimum Wages in Europe?, in: ETUI Report, European Trade Union Institute, No. 124.

Salverda, W. (2010), The Netherlands – Minimum Wage Fall shifts Focus to Part-Time Jobs, in: Vaughan-Whitehead, D. (ed.): The Minimum Wage revisited in the enlarged EU, Geneva: International Labour Organization, pp. 299-339.

Scarpetta, S., Sonnet, A., Manfredi, T. (2010), Rising Youth Unemployment During the Crisis – How to Prevent Negative Long-Term Consequences on a Generation, in: OECD Social, Employment and Migration Working Papers, No. 106, Paris: OECD Publishing.

Schels, B. (2007), Jugendarbeitslosigkeit und psychisches Wohlbefinden, in: IAB Forschungsbericht, Institute for Employment Research, No. 13.

Schmid, B., Schulten, T. (2006), Der französische Mindestlohn SMIC, in: Schulten, T. (ed.): Mindestlöhne in Europa, Hamburg: VSA-Verlag, pp. 102-126.

Schmidt, K. (2008), Arbeitsmarktreform und Mindestlöhne – Ein Schritt vor, zwei Schritte zurück, in: ifo Schnelldienst, Special Issue, Vol. 61, No. 6, München: ifo Institut für Wirtschaftsforschung, pp. 21-23.

Schmillen, A., Umkehrer, M. (2013), The Scars of Youth Effects of Early-Career Unemployment on Future Unemployment Experiences, in: IAB Discussion Paper, Institute for Employment Research, No. 6.

Schneider, F. (2008), Mindestlöhne erzeugen Schwarzarbeit, in: ifo Schnelldienst, Special Issue, Vol. 61, No. 6, München: ifo Institut für Wirtschaftsforschung, pp. 31-33.

Schulten, T. (2006), Mindestlöhne in den BeNeLux-Staaten, in: Schulten, T. (ed.): Mindestlöhne in Europa, Hamburg: VSA-Verlag, pp. 71-101.

Schulten, T. (2012): WSI-Mindestlohndatenbank – Version March 2012, Hans Böckler Stiftung, March.

Schulten, T. (2013): WSI-Mindestlohnbericht 2013 – Anhaltend schwache Mindestlohnentwicklung in Europa, in: WSI-Mitteilungen, Vol. 2, pp. 125-132.

Shaviro, D. (1997), The Minimum Wage, the Earned Income Tax Credit, and Optimal Subsidy Policy, in: The University of Chicago Law Review, Vol. 64, No. 2, pp. 405-481.

Siebert, H. (2008), Der Mindestlohn setzt Anreize für mehr Arbeitslose, in: ifo Schnelldienst, Special Issue, Vol. 61, No. 6, München: ifo Institut für Wirtschaftsforschung, pp. 19-20.

Sinn, H.-W. (2008), Von einem Mindestlohn, den man nicht bekommt, kann man nicht leben – Ein Plädoyer für den besseren Sozialstaat, in: ifo Schnelldienst, Special Issue, Vol. 61, No. 6, München: ifo Institut für Wirtschaftsforschung, pp. 57-61.

Sinn, H.-W., Blum, U., Hüther, M., Schmidt, C., Snower, D., Straubhaar, T., Zimmermann, K. (2008), Mindestlohn – Für und Wider – Aufruf der Präsidenten und Direktoren der Wirtschaftsforschungsinstitute, in: ifo Schnelldienst, Special Issue, Vol. 61, No. 6, München: ifo Institut für Wirtschaftsforschung, pp. 3-4.

Skourias, N. (1992), Un Réexamen des Incidences du SMIC sur L'Emploi, la Participation et le Chômage des Jeunes, in: Centre d'Economie Régionale, Groupe de Recherches sur l'Internationalisation, la Formation et l'Emploi, No. 7, September.

Skourias, N. (1995), Salaire Minimum et Emploi des Jeunes – L'Experience Francaise, in: Benhayoun, G., Bazen, S. (eds.): Salaire Minimum et Bas Salaires, pp. 255-274.

SOEP (ed.) (2011), Socio-Economic Panel – Wave 2011, published by the German Institute for Economic Research (DIW).

SPD (ed.) (2013), Das Wir entscheidet – Regierungsprogramm 2013-2017, Press release 23.08.2013, http://www.spd.de/link ableblob/96686/data/20130415_regierungsprogramm_2013_ 2017.pdf [retrieved on 24.08.2013].

Stewart, M. (2002), The Impact of the Introduction of the UK Minimum Wage on the Employment Probabilities of Low Wage Workers, in:

Warwick Economic Research Papers, Department of Economics, No. 630.

Stewart, M. (2004), The Employment Effects of the National Minimum Wage, in: Economic Journal, Vol. 114, No. 494, pp. 110-116.

Stigler, G. (1946), The Economics of Minimum Wage Legislation, in: American Economic Review, Vol. 36, pp. 358-365.

Straubhaar, T. (2008), Mindestsicherung jenseits von Mindestlöhnen, in: ifo Schnelldienst, Special Issue, Vol. 61, No. 6, München: ifo Institut für Wirtschaftsforschung, pp. 40-42.

Streissler, E. (2008), Österreich braucht keine gesetzlich festgelegten Mindestlöhne, in: ifo Schnelldienst, Special Issue, Vol. 61, No. 6, München: ifo Institut für Wirtschaftsforschung, pp. 34-36.

Sturn, S. (2008), Beschäftigungseffekte des französischen Mindestlohns, in: Horn, G., Joebges, H., Logeay, C., Sturn, S. (eds.): Frankreich – Ein Vorbild für Deutschland? Ein Vergleich wirschaftspolitischer Strategien mit und ohne Mindestlohn, in: IMK Report, No. 31, pp. 22-25.

Turner, M., Demiralp, B. (2001), Do Higher Minimum Wages Harm Minority and Inner-City Teens?, in: Review of Black Political Economy, Vol. 28, No. 4, pp. 95-121.

Van Hemel, L., Darquenne, R. (2009), Een andere Kijk op Hardnekkige Jeugwerkloosheid – Aanbevelingen en Succesfactoren bij de Inschakeling van Laaggeschoolde Jongeren, Brussels: Koning Boudewijnstichting.

Van Soest, A. (1994), Youth Minimum Wage Rates – The Dutch Experience, in: International Journal of Manpower, Vol. 15, No. 2, pp. 100-117.

Vaughan-Whitehead, D. (2010), Minimum Wage Revival in the enlarged EU – Explanatory Factors and Developments, in: Vaughan-Whitehead, D. (ed.): The Minimum Wage revisited in the enlarged EU, Geneva: International Labour Organization, pp. 1-56.

Welch, F. (1969), Linear Synthesis of Skill Distribution, in: The Journal of Human Resources, Vol. 4, No. 3, pp. 311-327.

Welch, F. (1974), Minimum Wage Legislation in the United States, in: Economic Inquiry, Vol. 12, Iss. 3, pp. 285-318.

Williams, N., Mills, J. (2001), The Minimum Wage and Teenage Employment – Evidence from Time Series, in: Applied Economics, Vol. 33, Iss. 3, pp. 285-300.

List of Tables

1	The Effect of the MW in different Models	36
2	Youth (Un)Employment Rates and NEET Rates in Selected Countries	39
3	Cost of NEETs in Selected Countries in 2008 and 2011	47
4	Key Facts about different Youth Labor Markets and Minimum Wage Systems	57
5	Youth MWs and MW Fixing Machinery by Country	59
6	Proponents and Opponents of a legally binding MW in Germany	86
7	Share of Young Workers who might be affected from a MW	93
8	Disemployment Effects for Young Workers in case of different MWs	94
A.1	Tabular Summary of Results from French Literature	106
A.2	Tabular Summary of Results from Spanish Literature	110
A.3	Tabular Summary of Results from Greek Literature	112
A.4	Tabular Summary of Results from Portuguese Literature	113
A.5	Tabular Summary of Results from Belgian Literature	115
A.6	Tabular Summary of Results from Dutch Literature	117
A.7	Tabular Summary of Results from British Literature	118
A.8	Tabular Summary of Results from American Literature	120
A.9	Tabular Summary of Results from German Simulations	124
A.10	Tabular Summary of Results from German Studies concerning Sectoral MWs	128

List of Figures

1	Impact of a MW in the Neoclassical Model	20
2	The MW impact in the Neoclassical and in the Monopsony Model	22
3	MW and Employment under Monopsonistic Competition	25
4	Impact of a MW in a Two-Sector Model	27
5	Theoretical Wage Distribution with and without a MW	29
6	Comparison of Youth and Adult Unemployment Rate in OECD Area (2008)	82